"Gary Hawkins' book is outstanding! It delivers powerful insight into the measuring and managing of one's customer base. This book gives us a road map to organize our future around customers rather than product. Gary is truly a leader in the industry!"
— **Chuck McNett**, Director of Marketing
Niemann Foods

"Gary Hawkins is uniquely qualified to characterize the retail customer. His innovative operational ideas and leading edge thinking have allowed him to convert information gained from customers' shopping experiences to a successful and profitable business tool. Gary's personal and professional abilities and experience are effectively demonstrated in this book. *Building the Customer Specific Retail Enterprise* is a valuable source of information for store operators who want to take their businesses to the next level."
— **Charles B. Barcelona**, President, Retired
Peter J. Schmitt Co., Inc.

"*Building the Consumer Specific Retail Enterprise* is sure to become one of the very few textbooks available on this subject that has genuine credibility. Gary's unique experience as being the retailer who created many of the actions described in the book (already duplicated by numerous retailers around the world), makes this publication a reference that even those on the cutting edge will learn from."
— **Roger Morgan**, Morgan's IGA
Australia

"Gary Hawkins has written an important book which will help retailers understand, use and benefit from their investment in customer specific marketing. Today's technology components provide the vehicle to make it possible; however, it is only when retailers commit their organizations to be customer driven that it actually happens. This book describes very clearly what that commitment must be!"

— **Peter Wolf**, Vice President, Targeted Customer Marketing
Store Automated Systems, Inc.

"Gary Hawkins has written an essential book for the serious Frequent Shopper practitioner. It is a valuable resource from someone who has 'been there — done that.'"

— **Al Lees**, Chairman
Lees Supermarket

"Gary's book is a terrific source of ideas on how to use Customer Specific Marketing to grow your business. He has outlined some great examples of how retailers are using customer data to help them make better decisions in their businesses. Whether you are a beginner or have a mature club card program, this book will help you."

— **Bill Feldpausch**, Vice President, Sales & Marketing
Felpausch Food Centers

"For those embarking on a loyalty program, I highly recommend this book. It contains valuable insights that will help you successfully navigate this fascinating area of retailing."

— **Inaki Ereno**, Customer Marketing Director
Continente
Spain

"Gary is a pioneer in customer specific retailing and has written the must-have book for the retail industry. His worldwide consulting and hands-on retailing experience combine to make this an essential handbook for putting information-enabled retailing to work successfully."

— **Brian Woolf**, President,
Retail Strategy Center, Inc.
Author of *Customer Specific Marketing*

"Gary blends insightful and actionable tidbits with actual, results-oriented examples. This is not a book for the casual reader, but one for the practitioner!"

— **Thomas Murphy**, Vice President, Information Systems
The Kroger Company

"Gary's insights on the utilization of customer information to gain competitive advantage will have a profound impact on retailers and manufacturers alike. This book is a must for mass marketers looking to capitalize on information-enabled technology to better meet the needs of their consumers."
— **Laura M. Klauberg**, Director, Customer Specific Consumer Marketing
Unilever Home and Personal Care

"In today's hyper-competitive marketplace, consumer-driven management must be adopted. Gary Hawkins has demonstrated, by successful practices as a supermarket operator as well as a consultant, that his visionary strategies and tactics are right on track. In this book, Hawkins not only shares his clear vision of future retailing, but he presents hands-on experiences not available elsewhere."
— **Terry Aoki**, Group CIO — Living Essentials Group
Mitsubishi Corporation

"*Building the Customer Specific Retail Enterprise* is a practical, hands-on guide for any retailer who has the courage to embrace loyalty marketing. This book is like an owner's manual for supermarket retailers with frequent shopper card programs. For Baker's it is both a refresher course and a roadmap for the future!"
— **Stephen Zubrod**, Vice President of Marketing,
Baker's

Building the CUSTOMER SPECIFIC RETAIL ENTERPRISE

GARY E. HAWKINS

Dedication

To the associates and management team of Green Hills Farms who have so well endured the ongoing journey to customer specific retailing.

Particularly to John Mahar and Lisa Piron who have played a fundamental role in the development of customer specific retailing, and have helped educate me in the process.

To my father Keith, for being supportive as we have experimented at Green Hills.

To Brian Woolf for being a friend, educator and mentor. Traveling the globe would simply not be as much fun without meeting occasionally — in some city about the world — to enjoy a bottle of wine!

To my children who send me e-mail when I'm traveling and make it possible for me to do what I do.

And to my wife, Heather, for not only tolerating my passion with trying to change the world of retail, but actively supporting it.

BUILDING THE CUSTOMER SPECIFIC RETAIL ENTERPRISE

Cover design and layout by The WDBurdick Company

Editing by Paula Hawkins and Leslye Wood

Library of Congress Cataloging-in-Publication Data
99-90664

ISBN: 0-9672562-0-8

Hawkins, Gary E.
Building the Customer Specific Retail Enterprise

Published by Breezy Heights Publishing, P.O. Box 46, Skaneateles, NY 13152, United States.

To order call: (US) 315.685.5175

Table of Contents

Foreword

It is always a pleasure to read a book by a successful pioneer. Gary Hawkins is such a person. He has been on the extreme leading edge of Customer Specific Marketing over the past five years. His store, Green Hills Farms, in Syracuse, New York, is one of the top five retailers in the world using the latest technology available to capture and use information. No other retailer has tested so many ways to differentiate customer offers, measuring the results at every step. Gary was the first retailer to run his business based on its customer profitability.

Not only does he provide us with insights from being a hands-on marketer, but also from his extensive work consulting with other retailers, of all sizes, around the world. The mixture of this cross-fertilization of practices and ideas makes this an essential handbook for retailers in all sectors.

The book covers Gary's latest thinking on the fundamentals of Customer Specific Marketing, with many interesting, fresh examples. It shows how customer information can be used to improve the efficiency of various parts of the business. It sets out a groundbreaking series of tables showing how customer and product information can be used effectively by customer managers, category managers and manufacturers.

Better information leads to better decision making. That's the real power of this new development in retailing. Retailers who choose not to capture their customer data place themselves at a disadvantage. This is the essential message that runs throughout. Become an information-enabled retailer, as Gary is often apt to say, and manage your destiny.

Brian Woolf

Brian Woolf, President of the Retail Strategy Center, Inc. Greenville, SC, is the author of Customer Specific Marketing *and consults with retailers around the world on this subject.*

Introduction

Imagine a retailer being able to offer different products at different prices to different customers all at the same time. Each individual customer receiving a mix of products and prices, services and privileges, information and recognition, all based upon the customer's preferences and needs. A retail business that measures sales, not by products sold, but by customers. A retail business that quantifies the value of its customer base — and knows it is a more valuable asset than its product inventory. A retail business organized around customers, not products. The customer specific retail enterprise.

The creation of such an enterprise is well under way. It is being powered by technology and the detailed customer information gathered through retail frequent shopper programs. Arising from the detailed customer information come new metrics to use in managing the retail enterprise. As retailers around the world discover the power of managing their businesses using these new measures, the retail industry is experiencing as fundamental a change as it did when the corner grocer gave way to the modern, self-service supermarket.

This change is impacting the entire retail supply chain. As retailers reorganize their businesses around their customers, rather than products, it is forcing the manufacturers and suppliers to review how they do business and go to market. Retailers can now measure the value of specific brands to their individual customers. No longer is mass marketing, one price for all, the most efficient and profitable way to go to market.

Worldwide, frequent shopper programs have to date been most prevalent in the supermarket channel, possibly due to the intense competition in this sector and a continual search for any possible margin improvement. Many of the concepts and examples used in this book are drawn from the supermarket and hypermarket channels but are equally applicable across almost all forms and sizes of retail. In my travels, I have spent time with people from the fast food industry, the hotel industry, and many other retail sectors. All have found value in the approach to business organization offered in this book. Perhaps the numbers change; but any retailing, to be successful, must have the customer at its core.

This book is not for retailers alone. As the evolution to true customer specific retailing continues, there are huge implications for other parts of the industry. There is a discussion in Chapter 11 that will be of particular interest to manufacturers, both consumer packaged goods companies and private label suppliers. As retailers begin to understand and use their customer data, it will impact heavily on their advertising and merchandising strategies.

The type of profound change offered by customer specific retailing can create great challenges or once-in-a-lifetime opportunities. Because of the confluence of two major, interrelated trends, the opportunity exists for the development of new strategies and the use of new tactics to fight the retail war. These two trends are the ever-decreasing cost of information technology, and the cost-effective gathering of detailed customer information that it enables.

As I travel about the world working with members of the retail industry, it is striking how few senior managers truly understand the implications that these trends portend for the retail industry. Too few companies understand the strategic implications of gathering, understanding, and using customer data.

For those executives and company leaders who do understand the role technology and customer information can play in reshaping the retail business, the times present a unique opportunity to upend the status quo and to position themselves for market leadership in the years to come.

Customer specific retailing is still in the early stages. We all have years of work ahead of us sorting and sifting through the enormous volumes of information that we gather about our customers, learning what's important and why customers behave the way they do. Those retailers who have already embarked on this journey are already out in front; laggards will find it increasingly difficult to catch up in this new race.

This book is meant to provide a profoundly different view of retail frequent shopper programs than is commonly put forth. The true power of these programs lies in the detailed customer information that is gathered when customers use their frequent shopper cards each time they shop. Too many retailers view this information as a by-product of their promotional efforts.

Many retailers, having launched their frequent shopper programs, are now casting about, looking for where to go next. They have vague notions about rewarding their best customers; many run some type of reward program without really knowing what to expect. It is hoped that this book will help provide some structure and direction for their efforts.

A few words of explanation...

The subject matter of this book is referred to by many names: loyalty marketing, frequent shopper programs, and customer specific marketing are but a few of them. I have chosen to use customer specific retailing simply because it is the most accurate in its description.

Retailers now have the capability to communicate and deliver differentiated offers and information to individual customers.

This book is arranged around the theme of building a new retail enterprise, a retail enterprise organized around customer information.

Section One, "Surveying the Site," takes a look at what has been learned so far in the area of frequent shopper programs around the globe. It sets the stage for the creation of the customer specific retailing enterprise.

Section Two, "Building the Foundation," addresses what is necessary for retailers to begin capturing extremely high levels of detailed customer information through their cards and maintaining this in some type of database or data warehouse.

Section Three, "Building the New Enterprise Structure," focuses on creating the structure for customer specific retailing. Using the vast amounts of customer information discussed in Section Two, new communication tools, organizational structure, and new metrics can now be developed for use in measuring and managing our retail businesses.

Section Four, "Shopping and Working in the New Retail Enterprise," speaks to how the new retail enterprise operates, its marketing and operational strategies. This is the fun section, and includes many examples from retailers about how they are using their customer information.

Section Five, "Where To Next," pulls together all the preceding material to show how retailers can evolve to true customer specific retailing and yield management.

Section Six, the "Conclusion," presents the state of the industry relative to frequent shopper programs around the world, and closes with some additional thoughts regarding the future of customer specific retailing.

While writing this book, I was presented with the challenge of how to refer to different customer groups. Using the terms "higher-spending" and "lower-spending" becomes somewhat cumbersome and not altogether accurate for describing different groups of customers. I decided to use the designations "gold," "silver," "bronze," and "tin" to connote different levels of customers as these seem to be universally understood — "gold" being the highest spending customers, "tin" the lowest-spending customers.

These terms are used generically in some places, and in others, they refer to specific categories of customers. Where the terms are used generically, for example "gold" meaning higher-spending customers, I have placed the term in quote marks. Where the term refers to a specific customer category, I have capitalized the name, for example Gold customers (those who spend on average more than $100 a week).

In addition, you will encounter other names used to refer to different categories of customers. In Chapter Five, "Customer Category Management," I have used the terms "whales," "starfish," "cod," and "sharks" to connote different customer groups. This was done as part of an analogy used in that particular chapter to help explain the variances in the composition of retailers' customer bases.

Green Hills Farms uses gemstones to describe its customer groups. You will see Diamond, Ruby, Pearl, and Opal used to refer to different groups. Diamond customers are the highest-spending group, Rubies the next highest-spending, and so on.

There is an additional point to be addressed: the issue of consumer privacy. Customer specific retailing, by definition, implies a knowledge and understanding of individual customers' purchasing habits. While this can be construed as having Orwellian "big brother" overtones, I believe that retailers can and should treat this information respectfully; indeed, retailers have an obligation to do so. Individuals are becoming more and more concerned about their personal information — rightfully so, when more and more personal information is being captured in databases beyond most peoples' knowledge, and "identity theft" becomes a more common crime.

I believe that this issue involves some type of compromise, either stated or implied. A great majority of retailers take the safeguarding of their customer data very seriously and strongly enforce their policies governing its use. At the same time, customers are usually willing to exchange their information for value. In the case of customer specific retailing, that "trade" implies the customer receiving offers, services, and privileges that are valuable to him or her individually, in return for allowing the retailer to capture the customer's purchasing data.

I think it is important to note that I am a retailer. As CEO of Green Hills Farms, I am in the position of being able to practice what I preach. Green Hills Farms is an independent supermarket located in Syracuse, New York. A fourth generation family business, Green Hills is a high volume store, with double the industry average sales per square foot.

We began our journey in customer specific retailing in early 1993. Through trial and error, a supportive management team, a willingness to experiment with new technology, and a persistent drive, we have made great strides in unlocking the power hidden in the gigabytes of customer data stored on our computers.

As President of DataWorks Marketing Group, I spend the majority of my time working with other members of the retail industry, both large and small, around the world. Seeing other retailers successfully launching their programs, and experiencing gains to their profit margins in a short period of time, simply reinforces my faith in the power of customer specific retailing.

I have tried throughout the book to incorporate examples from retailers around the world. There are, of course, many examples from Green Hills Farms. Green Hills operates at the leading edge in this evolution to true customer specific retailing; other advanced practitioners are finding success in similar areas. Are these practices successful? Do they make sense? Judge for yourself.

By combining a real world knowledge of how retail operates on the sales floor, with a consultant's view of the theories and retail practices around the world, I hope that I can bring some value to your thinking and efforts in the frequent shopper arena. My experience as a retailer, launching and operating a frequent shopper card has brought me to this point. I have seen firsthand the power of information based retailing — how detailed customer information can truly change the way a retailer is organized and operates.

I am continuously learning. I encourage anyone with other thoughts, ideas, and experiences to contact me with comments relative to this book and the information presented. My e-mail address is: ghawkins@dataworksmktg. com.

Customer specific marketing has forever changed the retail industry. The traditional retail economic model of "one price for all" is dead; the new economics is simply too powerful. Technology has wrought this change and it has only just begun; the age of true one-to-one marketing is here. To get from here to there — from decades of mass marketing to true customer specific marketing — requires a great deal of change in the way we as retailers do business. This is not always comfortable change; successful customer specific retailing requires going to market differently.

This is a time of great danger and exciting opportunity for the retail industry. Danger from other retail formats devouring existing channels. Danger from internet based companies completely changing the rules. Exciting opportunity because now, for the first time, retailers can organize their businesses around their customers, form relationships with them, and thrive. The choice is ours.

Section 1: Surveying the Site

Since the advent of self-service retailing more than sixty years ago, the retail industry has been organized around products. Self-service supermarkets, drug stores, discount stores, and others were built on the premise of displaying products that people could shop for themselves. Product was king. Retail sales were measured by how many and what products were sold. Inventory was an asset to be managed. The advent of scanning took this product measurement to a new level. Retailers further honed their merchandising skills by measuring product movement far more accurately. Retailers became masters of product logistics.

Mass merchandising retail is nearing the end of its present evolution. Consolidation is the game now, with the largest players growing even larger to maximize the efficiencies of their product based business structure. The result: too many stores chasing too few people. Mass retail has gone global — the same stores, same merchan-

dise found in cities around the world. At the same time, technology is driving us in the opposite direction, leading us to the individual customer, to customizing products and the shopping experience.

A new form of retailing is now appearing on the evolutionary scene. Retailing truly organized around the customer. Sales measured by customer, not by products. No longer product inventory, but customer inventory. Share of customer rather than share of market. Product shrink giving way to customer shrink. A new retail enterprise built upon a foundation of customer information: customer specific retailing.

What has brought this about? Computers and simple plastic cards — frequent shopper cards. For the first time, retailers can now measure customer behavior with the data gathered through retail frequent shopper programs. A handful of retailers around the globe have moved far beyond viewing their programs as simply another marketing or promotional effort. They have learned that it is far more profitable to organize themselves around the gathering, understanding, and use of detailed customer information. These are the companies evolving into customer specific retailers.

Surveying the Site

Chapter 1: Laying the Groundwork

Technology has enabled retailers to cost-effectively launch and operate loyalty programs. World-class practitioners are identifying more than 90% of their sales, week in and week out, and more than 75% of all transactions are done with the retailers frequent shopper cards. These are the companies that realize the retail battleground has shifted. Information is the new field of battle, technology and information systems are the new weaponry.

This, combined with a constant search for profit improvements, has led to an explosion of frequent shopper programs around the world. Retailers everywhere are having an increasingly difficult time maintaining sizeable sales and profit increases. They are beginning to realize that they now need to focus their efforts on improving the profit yield from the customers they already have in their stores.

This has led nearly 10,000 supermarkets in the United States alone to have some type of frequent shopper card program. In addition, thousands of retail stores throughout Europe have some type of loyalty program. Australia,

New Zealand, and Japan are all ready to explode. Retailers around the world are discovering that there is a better, more profitable way to go to market.

Why a new way of practicing retail? Retailers have discovered that all their customers are not equal in value; therefore, one price for all is no longer the most profitable marketing proposition.

Brian Woolf, in his groundbreaking study, "Measured Marketing," found startling surprises in the customer data held by supermarkets around the world. Some of the major findings: the top 30% of customers ranked by sales provide 75% of a retailer's annual sales volume. Conversely, the bottom 30% of customers provide less than 3% of annual sales (refer to Figures 1-1 and 1-2). The obvious point here is that all of a retailer's customers

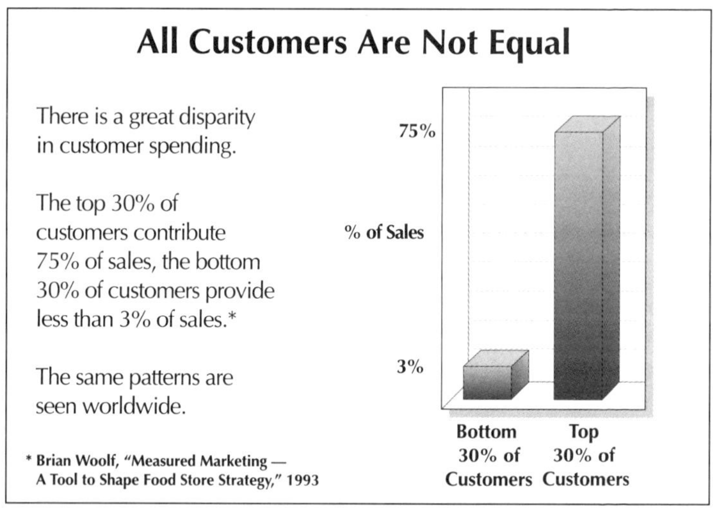

Figure 1-1

are not equal in value. There are major differences between our customers as evidenced by Woolf's data. The fascinating part is that these numbers hold true within a few points around the world — large retailer or small, U.S., France, Australia, or Japan. It does not matter.

Let's take this a step further. Additionally, what has been found is that, along with our customers being unequal in their purchasing, there is also a large difference in the rewards they have been receiving from us!

The pyramid on the left, shown in Figure 1-3, represents a retailer's customers. The top 30% (based on spending) are generating approximately 75% of annual sales; the bottom 30%, less than 3% of sales. The pyramid on the right represents a retailer's marketing rewards. Marketing

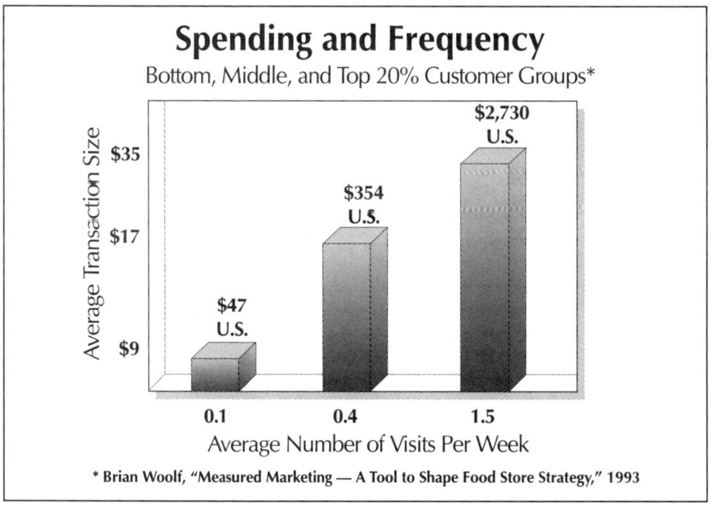

Figure 1-2

rewards here are defined as a retailer's total markdown expense, in addition to marketing and promotional expenditures.

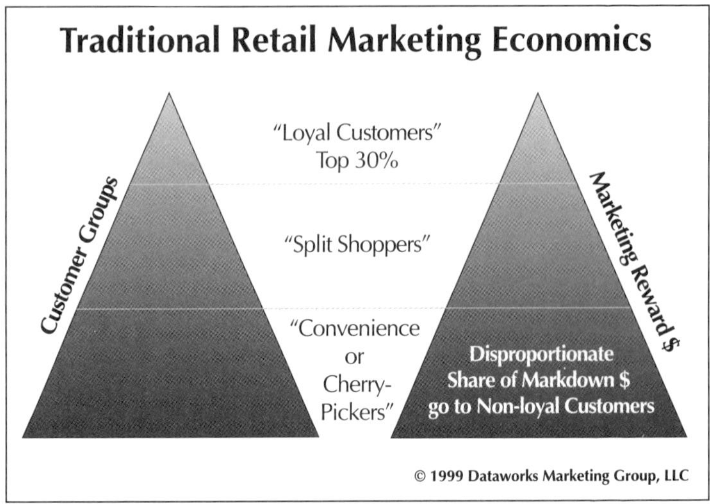

Figure 1-3

As we can see, the top customers are typically receiving a disproportionately small share of these rewards. The bottom customers, those giving us very little in sales, are receiving a disproportionately large share of the retail marketing rewards.

Retailers having customer information, and willing to go to market differently than in the past, can dramatically change this situation. These retailers can invert this equation. As can be seen in Figure 1-4, these retailers can now provide more proportional rewards to their higher-spending customers. They do this not by spending more; rather, they redirect their existing expenditures. They withdraw some of the rewards to the low-spending customers, and redirect these rewards to the higher-spending customers.

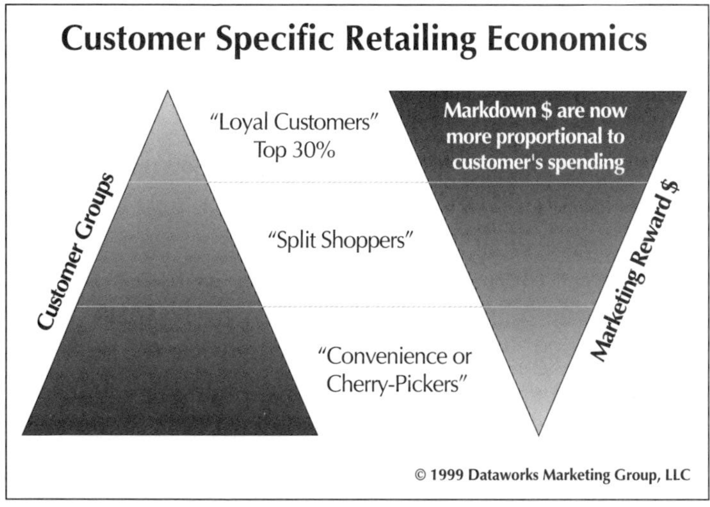

Figure 1-4

Let's take a real world example of how this can work. Supermarket operators in the U.S. have for decades sold Thanksgiving turkeys far below cost in the hopes of luring customers in to do their holiday shopping. Anyone could walk into a store and buy a turkey at a price far below cost. And indeed, almost every supermarket had cherry pickers who would come in, buy a turkey, and leave, giving the store a pure loss on that transaction.

One retailer, Green Hills Farms, decided to try and change that situation. In the fall of 1994, rather than sell turkeys far below cost to anyone who walked in, Green Hills decided to give them away free to their best customers. The program was quite simple: all shoppers spending more than $500 in the 10 weeks prior to Thanksgiving, using their Green Hills frequent shopper cards, would receive a free, fresh turkey, any size they wished. Green Hills simply redirected their rewards to the higher-spending customers.

What happens as a retailer begins to change its reward structure, inverting the pyramid? Several things: 1) the retailer begins to retain these higher-spending customers better than in the past; 2) these customers begin rewarding the retailer with even more spending; 3) as this occurs, profit margins improve because these customers are purchasing more products at full price; and, 4) the retailer begins attracting other high-spending customers due to the rewards offered.

For example, the first free Thanksgiving turkey program run by Green Hills resulted in substantial changes in customer shopping behavior. The impact was eye opening — a gain of more than 20% in the number of customer households spending over the $500 threshold, compared to the same 10-week period the year before, a gain of more than 1% to our gross margins — *all within 10 weeks.*

One price for all is no longer the most profitable retail pricing strategy. Every retailer has customers who spend more than others, customers who are more profitable than others. Historically, it has been the higher-spending customers who have provided the profits to subsidize the cherry pickers! This can now be changed.

Indeed, experience has shown that those retailers who differentiate the most realize the most substantial profit margin improvements. It is not uncommon now for supermarket retailers with good programs to realize a gain of 1% to 2% in their gross profit margins. A smaller number of retailers have experienced even more significant gains: 4% to 5% gains in gross profit margins. Some retailers have doubled their bottom line profitability; one regional supermarket chain in the U.S. has tripled its net profit. This is what customer specific retailing is all about.

The retail industry is moving toward yield management: different prices for different customers to achieve a better return on investment for our marketing expenditures. This really should not be such a strange notion to retailers; other industries have been doing it for some time. The airlines are masters of yield management, selling seats on the same plane for different prices at different times to different customers. It is a well-accepted practice. Credit card companies do the same thing, altering their interest rates for different customers, based on the customers' payment histories and potential value to the card issuer. In effect, insurance companies do the same thing. Different people pay different rates for their automobile insurance, based on their driving records, age, sex, and other factors.

Technology is driving this change in the retail industry. Technology makes it possible for retailers to cost-effectively capture huge amounts of information relative to their customers' shopping behavior. Technology is also allowing retailers to communicate cost-effectively with individual customers, and to electronically deliver customer specific offers and rewards to them at the checkout.

There is no going back. The pace of technological advancement is ever increasing, while the costs are continuously decreasing. Mankind has never given up a technology once it has been acquired. We need look no further than the controlled use of fire, or even the original stone tools used by prehistoric man. Both were, for generations, continuously refined and adapted for use. Even nuclear technology, originally developed for warfare, is now being used to provide electrical power to millions of people worldwide.

Retailers today need to be customer focused, not product driven. When I speak at various conferences, I ask the retailers in the audience to tell me the most important part of their businesses. Inevitably, the answer is "the customer." But by probing just beneath the surface, it becomes obvious that the majority of retailers simply pay lip service to the customer. Their organizations are really built around the product side of the business, and the efforts of their personnel are directed at maximizing advertising monies, slotting fees, and other such things.

This is being product driven. Slotting fees dictate which products will be carried — not the customer. Advertising monies dictate which items appear on the front page of the advertising circular — not the customer's choice or preference. Think how much more enticing we as retailers could be if we advertised the products and services that our highest spending customers really wanted.

I travel a great deal, and so I belong to many of the airline frequent flier programs. One day I received in the mail three offers from three different airlines, none of which was my primary airline. Each of these offers was the same; each promised me 5,000 bonus miles if I changed my long distance telephone service over to MCI. Now, who was the winner in this promotion? The airlines or MCI? What is the difference between this example and customers opening their Sunday papers and seeing several competing supermarket advertisements, all selling Coke at about the same price? Who is the winner, the retailer or Coke?

To be successful in this new world of retailing requires a substantial shift in thinking. Many existing retailers will not be able to make the leap, as decades of product centered thinking poses too large a challenge for them to overcome. Customer specific retailing implies profound change for the industry, particularly for the packaged goods manufacturers, necessitating a change in the way they go to market.

Where there are challenges, there are opportunities. One of the most progressive packaged goods manufacturers is already exploring the best way to partner with retailers who have good customer databases, and the necessary customer communication and delivery infrastructure, to explore true customer specific marketing, based on customers' purchasing habits. We are seeing that many of the same principles that customer specific marketing is built upon at the retail level, are equally applicable to the marketing of brands in our stores.

It is very difficult for a retailer of any size to go from decades of mass marketing to true customer specific retailing overnight. Looking around the world, we see more of an evolution, rather than a revolution, occurring, as shown in Figure 1-5.

In the first stage, we see retailers launching their frequent shopper or loyalty programs. Typically, these programs require using the card in order for the customer to receive the advertised specials or some type of points program. Essentially, retailers are creating a two-tier pricing schedule in their stores: a discounted price for customers who use the card; full price for those who don't. A points program can accomplish the same thing. Both these strategies will be discussed in greater detail in the next section.

Customer Specific Retailing Evolution

Mass Marketing → True Customer Specific Marketing

Stage 1	Stage 2	Stage 3	Stage 4
Implement card program	Continue differentiation through various programs	Customer Category Management	True 1:1 marketing
First level of differentiation			Tailor the mix of products, prices, services and privileges to the customer
All price reductions require card	Skew rewards to more loyal customers	Expenses matched to revenue streams	Maximize customer profitability

Figure 1-5

In the second stage, we see retailers begin to skew the rewards to the higher-spending customers. This typically takes the form of different marketing programs that reward customers for achieving certain spending thresholds. The bottom line here is the same regardless of the program specifics — skewing the rewards to the higher-spending customers (inverting the pyramid).

In the third stage, leading practitioners are moving into customer category management. This is the segmenting of the customer base along economic, not demographic lines. As retailers begin to do this, they can begin to align their marketing expenditures with the income streams offered by the different categories of customers. This concept will be covered in much more depth in Sections Two and Three.

In the fourth stage, we see retailers evolving into true customer specific retailing; providing an assortment of products, prices, services, privileges, and information to individual customer households with the goal of maximizing their lifetime value to the retailer. Think of it as each customer having his or her own advertised specials each week...*and each customer's specials are different.* You may wonder how this can happen in a retail setting with tens of thousands, hundreds of thousands, or even millions of customer transactions a week. This is not science fiction. The technology to do this is here today, and is being implemented by forward thinking retailers around the world.

Though the technology exists, the majority of retailers, including some of those installing such technology, do not know what to do with it. There are far too many retailers, of all sizes around the globe, who have built customer information databases or data warehouses, but do not realize what they have. Perhaps they are overwhelmed by the sheer amount of data they have. Perhaps they do not know what to focus on. These retailers have an unused asset, one that can propel them to greater profitability and into customer specific retailing.

It has taken the better part of ten years for customer specific marketing to develop to its present level in the supermarket industry. We will see it cascade much more quickly through other retail channels. National chain drug stores, such as CVS and Rite Aid, are committed to being national with their card programs. Discounters, such as K-Mart and Target, are experimenting with programs. And even McDonalds is evaluating the use of different loyalty schemes around the world. There is no going back.

Peter Drucker, one of the preeminent management thinkers of the past several decades, discusses the revolution coming to retail in his book *Managing in a Time of Great Change*. The chapter entitled "The Information Revolution in Retail" begins to address the profound change occurring in logistics and the industry structure, due to the information explosion and the internet.

The years ahead, as retailers gather more detailed information and learn more about our customers' shopping behavior, herald a time of great change. Retailing is becoming as much about technology as it is about customer service. As Drucker so aptly puts it, "The changes are having profound effects on advertising, on consumer goods manufacturers, and on the structure of the economy. Retailing — rather than manufacturing or finance — may be where the action is now."

Section 2: Building the Foundation

Customer information is the lifeblood of the new retail enterprise. Like the foundation of a large building, the foundation must be solid and strong enough to support the structure built upon it. As with any building, the foundation must be maintained. This should not be viewed as a one-time project; constant monitoring and maintenance is required. Without quality data, the foundation will crack and the building fall. It is critical that this maintenance be regularly carried out at the deepest levels of the organization, the front lines at store level.

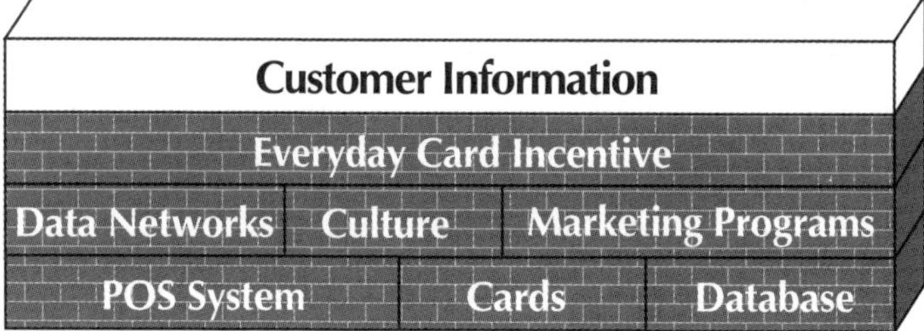

There is a great irony in the area of frequent shopper programs around the world: far too many retailers, of all sizes, have gotten it backwards. They view the information gathered through a card program as a by-product of their marketing efforts, not as the goal! These retailers believe that frequent shopper cards simply enable new types of marketing promotions: point gathering, electronic discounts, card-based sweepstakes, and so on. These companies believe that these types of promotions constitute a successful card program. But this is just the beginning! It is the information captured through the card that is the hidden treasure.

The primary purpose of a frequent shopper program is as an information gathering tool, not as a marketing or promotion program. A card based program provides a conduit to the customer. It is a tool to help the retailer identify and communicate with the customer, and ultimately, for the customer to communicate with the retailer.

Too many retailers simply layer their frequent shopper efforts onto their existing operations. In doing so, they increase their operating expenses, thereby negating the profit gains that can be realized. Successful, world-class practitioners re-direct their expenditures and make their customer specific retailing efforts central to their businesses.

Many retailers around the world are doing some of the things discussed in this section. World-class practitioners realize that it takes many of these factors in combination to create the strongest foundation. Just as concrete is a mixture of water, sand, and gravel, the customer specific retailer adjusts the mix of incentives, technology, and culture to provide the highest level of quality data possible.

We have seen retailers in several markets consciously making the choice not to have a card program because their competitors already have one. They are taking the path of differentiating themselves by positioning their shopping experience as being an easier one — due to not having to use a card. While this may be a legitimate strategy, I do not believe these retailers are taking a long-term view of the situation. In the long run, as Brian Woolf is fond of saying, "information is much more profitable than ignorance."

We have only to look at another industry to see the changes technology has wrought. The internet is bringing about major changes to the way cars are sold. A recent article stated that more than 50% of automobile buyers will have first checked the internet for information on the car they wish to purchase. Not only can consumers check safety information, competing models, and so on, but they can now learn what the car cost the dealer; indeed, it is possible to purchase a car over the internet at a fixed fee over the dealer invoice amount. Certainly this is creating great pressure on car dealers' profit margins, and is bringing tremendous change to the way cars are sold.

Retailers today with customer databases hold within their organizations the power to shift the playing field, to remake their industry. The balance of power has shifted to the retail side, away from the manufacturers and suppliers; yet most retailers do not realize the power of their customer information.

Building the Foundation

Chapter 2: Gathering the Information

With the development of bar codes and scanning technology, the retail industry was forever changed. Retailers now had the ability to track product movement much more efficiently and accurately through the supply chain. In addition, this technology allowed the development of entire systems within the retail industry; things such as product category management, efficient consumer response, and a host of others. All of these things would have been impossible if not for product scanning.

Indeed, product based information is the foundation for much of what is reported in a company's financial statements. From sales information to inventory management, scanning has provided retailers with vast amounts of information central to their operations. In short, modern retail could not function without scanning data.

Imagine now that we can scan our customers. As product scan data has wrought great change in retail operations, so too will customer scan data. All we are doing with frequent shopper cards is bar coding and scanning our customers.

Marketing programs and incentive schemes that are run through a frequent shopper card serve a dual role. First and foremost, they serve as an incentive for customers to identify themselves each time they shop, thereby allowing the retailer to capture detailed customer information. Secondly, these incentives may begin to change customer shopping behavior, encouraging customers to centralize their shopping with a specific retailer in return for specified rewards and offers.

In this section of the book, we are more concerned with the incentive programs as they enable information gathering. Advanced practitioners view marketing programs as useful in changing customers' shopping behavior. This will be discussed in depth in Chapter 10.

Given that the goal is to capture more than 90% of sales through the card, the question then becomes what incentive(s) will prove powerful enough to encourage customers to identify themselves each time they shop, by using their cards? The choice of this underlying incentive scheme must be strategic in nature and at the same time be cost-effective, so as not to burden the retailer with additional overhead.

In return for customers using their cards to identify themselves, the retailer must provide some type of value. Looking around the world, we see two fundamental methods of encouraging card use: price and points.

In the United States, the vast majority of retailers tie their frequent shopper card to their price reductions (advertised specials and other markdown items). This tactic accomplishes several things. Because the retailers had markdown prior to their card program, they have added no new operating costs by requiring their frequent shopper card for the customer to receive any of their advertised specials. This begins to provide a strong incentive for customers to get and to use the retailer's frequent shopper card every time they shop; in return, the retailer begins to capture a great amount of customer information.

This tactic also provides other benefits to the retailer. Typically, when a discount is tied to a frequent shopper card, the amount of the discount and the total of all the discounts received in that transaction are shown on the bottom of the customer's receipt. By moving all price reductions to the card, the retailer can show the customer exactly how much he or she is saving by shopping with the company and using the frequent shopper card.

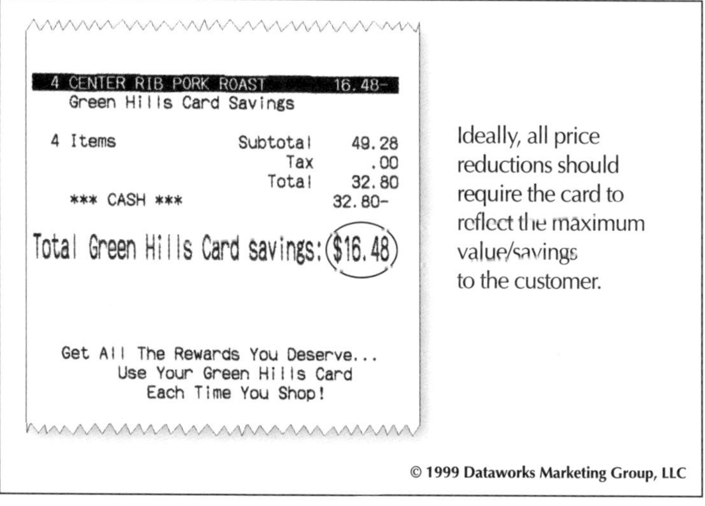

Ideally, all price reductions should require the card to reflect the maximum value/savings to the customer.

© 1999 Dataworks Marketing Group, LLC

Figure 2-1

This is a very simple thing, but very powerful. Many retailers show customers how much they save when purchasing an advertised item by stating the savings next to the sale price in their ad. Other retailers also show the savings on the sign at the display in the store. All this is forgotten, however, when the customer checks out and spends $100. That customer is walking out the door thinking about all the money he or she has just spent. By showing the discounts on the receipt and totaling them at the bottom, the customer now checks out and thinks about the money that he or she has just saved. Simple but powerful.

This strategy effectively creates a two-tier pricing schedule: those customers without a card pay full retail price; those with a card receive the specials. Even leading retailers who are capturing 90% of their total sales on the card now have 10% of their volume at full margin.

Throughout Europe and other parts of the world, the use of a points program is the preferred incentive for encouraging customers to use their frequent shopper cards. In many European countries, retailers are prohibited by law from selling the same item at different prices to different customers. There is also commonly a cultural aversion to the price differentiation that is practiced in the U.S. Points programs have developed as a way for these retailers to begin differentiating between customers; the highest-spending customers accumulate points, and the accompanying rewards, faster than lower-spending customers.

There are many variations of points programs around the world, but the basic premise is the same: customers earn points for each dollar (or peseta, franc, etc.) they spend. These points are then redeemed for some type of reward, typically either discount vouchers or gifts.

Points programs can be either ongoing or fixed length promotions. We will deal with the ongoing points programs here; fixed length promotions will be discussed in Chapter 10, along with other marketing programs.

Ongoing points programs are usually constructed as a 1% rebate scheme. Customers earn one point for each dollar spent; and they receive a discount certificate for every so many points earned. The discount is equivalent to 1% of the spending.

Tesco's loyalty scheme in the U.K. is an example of a traditional points program. Customers earn one point for each pound they spend; and they receive a £2.50 discount voucher for every £250 in accumulated purchases.

Traditional points programs, such as the Tesco program, are very expensive to operate. The retailer is now in effect rebating 1% of purchases back to the customer in the form of the discount vouchers. On top of this expense, there is the cost of mailing or distributing the vouchers. Additionally, there are the costs of handling these vouchers at the point of sale, and the follow-up bookkeeping. All in all, the retailer must generate a substantial sales and profit increase to justify the cost of this type of program.

Another form of points program is the points and partners program. The SuperClub loyalty program, organized and operated by SuperQuinn of Dublin, Ireland, is a much more complex, integrated partners scheme. Customers earn points based on their spending at any of the SuperQuinn supermarkets. But in addition, they can earn points based on their purchasing at any of 18 or so other partner merchants. These partners include Texaco petrol stations, hotels, etc. This point accumulation with other partners is generated electronically. They have put the necessary computer equipment in place at each of the partners' locations to swipe the customer's card and transfer the information on a regular basis to the master database at SuperClub head offices.

Points and partners programs are not the province of large retailers alone. Morgan's IGA in Australia, is a five-store, independent supermarket operator. Their ESP (Extra Savings Power) card program is also a points based program; customers earn points based on their spending. Morgan's also wanted to develop a partners program, but lacked the computer infrastructure to do this electronically. Morgan's got around this problem by creating ESP "stamps" worth five, 10, or 20 points. They would then sell these stamps to other partner merchants, who would in turn reward their customers with the ESP stamps. Customers simply bring the stamps to any Morgan's store, where they are scanned at the point of sale and the points added to their accounts.

Unfortunately, too many retailers choose schemes that sound like wonderful marketing programs, but simply will not generate enough information to be useful in moving to customer specific retailing. I spent a day with a large retailer in South America who had recently made the decision to take part in an air miles program. Customers shopping at this retailer and other partners would earn points based on their purchasing, that could be redeemed for discounted or free air travel. This retailer wished to use this card based program as their leaping-off point into customer specific retailing, but found out that it simply would not provide enough information.

This retailer faced several problems. First, it was not their program; they were simply a partner in a scheme operated by a third party. As such, they did not control the customer information — the real value. They would only receive limited reports once a month. This type of program — air miles — only appeals to a certain customer niche; not everyone desires free air travel. It is not a strong enough incentive to permit the retailer to identify the high levels of sales and transactions needed for customer specific retailing.

There is an important point to be made here. Far too many retailers, of all sizes around the world, view the above types of programs, be they price or points based, as the beginning and end of their frequent shopper efforts. They feel that this type of benefit alone will generate an increase in sales, profits, and customer loyalty. These programs simply provide the incentive for customers to identify themselves each time they shop. It is the information captured that is the gold mine for the retailer.

Retailers should be cautious in forecasting any sizeable sales increase directly from launching a frequent shopper program. For those retailers who do see a gain, it typically has more to do with the promotion, special prices, and events that accompany the launch, than it does with the card itself. My experience viewing frequent shopper programs around the world is this: if the retailer is first in their market with a strong program, they may realize some increase in sales simply due to the novelty. I have seen sales increases from 1-2% up to a high of nearly 20%. If the retailer is second or later in their market with a card, they are best advised to be cautious in planning for any type of substantial sales increase.

Retailers must break out of their "more sales" mentality. Almost every retailer around the world is looking for a silver bullet — some marketing program that will, overnight, increase sales and profits. This is short-term thinking, and, for the most part, not a winning strategy. To be successful in building the new retail enterprise, the retailer must take a longer-term view, realizing that the value of a frequent shopper program lies in the information gathered. It is this information, and the understanding and use of it, that provides a long-term strategic advantage to those retailers who understand the power of it.

Certainly, any business must grow to survive and be successful. The understanding and use of customer information now provides a more sustainable way to build sales and profits over time. As we will discuss later in the book, the customer specific retailer can begin to build relationship loyalty among their customers, thus helping insulate, to a degree, pure price competition.

The fact that only minimal sales increases may be associated with launching a program, reinforces the notion that the incentives provided to encourage card use must be cost-effective for the retailer. In addition, the choice of this primary incentive must be strategic. Simply offering a "me too" program will not do it. Just as in war, the choice of strategy must be based on the landscape, the physical and mental capabilities of the combatants, and the logistics. Translate this to the retailer's competition, technology, size, company culture, and so on.

What we have addressed above are the predominant choices for an everyday, underlying incentive to encourage customer card use. Experience has been that no one incentive remains powerful enough to capture upwards of 80%, let alone 90% or more, of sales on a regular basis. Attaining these levels usually requires multiple layers of values for the customer.

Customer acceptance and use of frequent shopper cards directly correlates to the values offered in the card.

Here are some of the other frequently used incentives for encouraging customer card use:

Sweepstakes

When Leevers supermarkets in Boulder, Colorado, launched their Leevers card program in the fall of 1997, they ran a sweepstakes for a new car. Customers received an entry in the drawing for the car each time they used their Leevers cards. This is a very powerful incentive for customers to sign up for, and use, a retailer's frequent shopper card.

The prize does not necessarily have to be this large. During Green Hills' anniversary sale in 1998, the store awarded a $100 gift certificate to a customer each week of the month-long event, with a grand prize of a year's supply of free groceries.

Wegmans, one of the premier regional supermarket operators in the U.S., ran a sweepstakes through their Shoppers Club card during Superbowl season. The prize: two tickets to the Superbowl, including hotel and travel.

Many retailers are given merchandise from vendors to use in promotions. These items can range from t-shirts and coolers to washing machines, televisions, and cars. Rather than run an in-store sweepstakes with paper entries, why not move the promotion into the card? Many of the database products offer a sweepstakes event capability. They will track the entries and randomly generate a winning number.

Reward Programs

By running some type of reward program through their frequent shopper card, the retailer is providing yet another layer of value to encourage customers to use their cards, identifying themselves when they shop. These types of programs can play an important role in boosting identification rates.

A reward program is typically a fixed-length, short-term promotion, promising some reward to the customer in return for spending at specific thresholds during the promotion.

An example of this type of program is provided by Price Chopper in Schenectady, New York. Customers spending at specified levels during a twelve-week program period can earn varying levels of discount certificates, which they can then use on future shopping orders. For example, a Price Chopper customer spending over $1,000 during this promotion would earn a 20% discount certificate, which could then be used on a future shopping trip.

It is not uncommon for a retailer to see a substantial lift in identification rates when running a strong reward program, causing their identification rate to climb from, for example, 80% to 85%, or even higher. Because these programs are not ongoing, they provide only a sporadic lift to card use — another reason why the everyday, underlying incentive scheme is so important. By running several reward programs over the course of the year, the retailer is helping to build the card use habit among its customers.

Donation Programs

Many retailers make charitable donations to organizations over the course of the year. A number of retailers have ongoing donation programs. For example, customers may give their register receipts to their favorite charity to turn in to the retailer for a donation rebate. We see the more successful retailers channeling their donation programs through their frequent shopper cards, providing yet another layer of value for their customers — just one more reason for customers to get and use the retailer's frequent shopper program.

Donation programs done through a frequent shopper program can take many forms.

Green Hills Farms ran a receipt based church rebate program. Customers would save their receipts and turn them in to their churches. The churches would then periodically bundle them up and turn them in to Green Hills for a "rebate" of 1% of the total purchases. This was a very successful program for more than 25 years.

In 1995, the program ended, and a card based program took its place. That year, Green Hills ran a nine-month church rebate promotion through the Green Hills frequent shopper card. Customers were asked to sign up for the program, letting the store know which churches they wished their donations to go to. Customers were told that Green Hills would rebate 1% of their total purchases made with their Green Hills cards during the nine months, provided they spent a minimum of $250 with the store. The program was well-received by both the churches and the customers. It made their lives easier as they no longer had to save receipt tapes or turn them in. That year, Green Hills donated more than $25,000 to area churches.

This type of program has now been run by a number of retailers around North America. Recipients have included churches, schools, and many other charitable organizations. The retailer is simply providing the fundraising vehicle for the charities and the customers; it is up to them to run with it.

Yet another way of approaching a donation program is to issue certificates directly to the customers, who give them to their charities of choice, who in turn redeem the certificates for the actual donation from the retailer. But again, this is done through the retailer's card program. For example, customers are told that during the next two months, the retailer will issue charitable certificates to them in the amount of 2% of their spending during the two-month program. At the end of the program, the retailer, using their database, generates a list of all the qualifying customers and their spending. They then mail "vouchers" to the customers in the amount of 2% of the customers' spending. The customers in turn donate the vouchers to the charities of their choice, who then redeem them with the retailer. These programs typically require a minimum expenditure by the customer during the program to qualify. The idea is to reward the higher-spending customers — not the cherry pickers — with more value.

Morgan's IGA, of Melbourne, Australia, has a rather novel twist on this theme. As many retailers are, Morgan's was constantly being barraged by groups seeking donations. Early on, they used this to help drive and establish their card program. People seeking a donation were told that indeed Morgan's would donate a percentage of their spending during a specified timeframe to their organization, provided they assisted with signing up a minimum of 10 new cardholders for Morgan's. How to turn donation requests into a "pay for performance" program!

Partners Programs

Partners programs can be as simple as a win-win program, or very complex with electronic networks to support them, as in the SuperClub program mentioned earlier.

Baker's of Omaha, Nebraska, has done an excellent job with its partners programs. Put together by Stephen Zubrod, Vice President of Marketing, they have included joint programs with the Nebraska Furniture Mart and the Omaha Royals baseball team.

At every Royals' Tuesday home game, Baker's cardholders receive four box seats for only $2 by showing their Baker's Value card at the box office. In addition, Baker's personnel scan the customers' Value cards at the entrance to the ballpark, and hold a sweepstakes during the game with different prizes.

During Tuesday evenings in February, Baker's cardholders receive special pricing at the Nebraska Furniture Mart. Baker's promotes the event heavily, usually pulling other vendors in as partners. Again, sweepstakes are run at the event and Baker's even uses the kitchen displays to showcase their prepared foods during the special evenings at the NFM.

Niemann Foods, a regional supermarket chain located in Illinois, has created an extensive partners program around its Max Saver card in the different markets in which it operates. For example, customers can save 20% on their dry cleaning by showing their Max cards at a certain dry cleaners. The Bank of Illinois offered a "no fees for one year" free checking account to cardholders. Niemann has over a dozen partners at any one time, periodically rotating in new partners and promotions.

These types of partner programs are typically win-win arrangements. The partner merchants extend a special offer to the retailer's cardholders in return for the retailer advertising their establishments under the umbrella of their program.

The goal of any type of partners program is quite simple: to create additional value for the customer and provide yet another reason for customers to obtain, carry, and use the retailer's frequent shopper card.

Everything that has been discussed in this section is dedicated to one goal: generating enough customer information so that the new retail enterprise can be built upon a strong foundation. The lesson to take away from this section is this: to move to capturing this level of customer information, channel all marketing and promotional programs through the frequent shopper card.

There are other ways of gathering detailed customer information. Customers paying by personal checks are essentially identifying themselves to a retailer. Co-branded credit card programs are another way that some retailers attempt to identify customers and begin building a database. Some retailers capture customer information as a part of their normal business. I once spoke to the owner of a chain of camera shops. They capture customer name, address, phone number, and what was purchased, through a warranty filled out with each camera sold. It is then a simple matter to enter this information into some type of database for marketing initiatives. Anyone purchasing a camera will need film, film development, and batteries.

Other retailers have similar opportunities. Jewelers or other luxury goods purveyors typically have a very high percentage of their sales paid for with credit cards. This offers another opportunity to begin building a customer database.

It really does not matter how a retailer gathers detailed customer information; the critical element is capturing enough of the total sales and transactions. The flaw in many of these other schemes is that they typically do not allow a retailer to capture anywhere near the needed volumes of information. One regional supermarket chain years ago let customers identify themselves by giving the cashier their telephone number. It did not take long for customers to realize that they could simply recite any number and it would allow them to receive their discounts. In addition, customers were moving and changing their telephone numbers. In all, this led to a corrupt database, one having a great deal of information, but no accurate way of tying it back to individual customers on a consistent basis.

To date, experience has been that it is only a well-constructed frequent shopper scheme that can succeed in capturing the necessary level of information, and consistently and accurately attributing it back to a specific customer. Perhaps in the future, we will simply ask our customers for their thumb prints, using biometric identification technology to identify them!

Building the Foundation

Chapter 3: Building Blocks

Before beginning to build our new retail enterprise, we must assemble the building blocks. As our new enterprise is built on detailed customer information, we must put in place the systems necessary to gather and analyze the information.

Technology is advancing at an ever increasing rate. What is written today will be out-of-date within months. What I will attempt to address here are the major points involved in the various components.

POS Systems

Perhaps the most basic component is the point of sale (POS) system. In addition to fulfilling its traditional duties (as the accounting tool for totaling what to charge customers and reporting sales), the POS system in our new enterprise must serve additional roles. Most basically, it must append to each transaction record the customer's identification — typically, his or her frequent shopper card number. The POS must collect and transfer transaction-level data to the database.

The following are some of the more important attributes a POS system should have to facilitate a frequent shopper program:

Discounts linked to card? In the United States, the majority of retailers link their discounts or markdowns to card use. To do this properly, a customer must present at the POS his or her frequent shopper card to receive any of the store's advertised specials or other items that are reduced in price. The customer or cashier must swipe the customer's card so that the POS reads it, linking card usage to discounts. When evaluating a new POS or upgrade to POS software to accommodate this, there are several additional questions that must be asked:

Can the customer's card be swiped at any point in the order? Some of the older POS systems required the customer card to be swiped before any items were scanned, or the customer would not receive any discounts on items scanned prior to the card swipe. While this is not impossible to work around, newer systems permit the scanning of the card at any stage of the order, thus improving customer throughput.

Customer specific pricing support? Will the POS system allow customer group specific pricing or true customer specific pricing? Almost all of the POS systems now on the market will allow two-tier pricing: regular price, and the discounted price with frequent shopper card. Several systems will allow several levels of pricing: regular price, and different prices on the same product for different categories of customers. The latest technology being used supports true customer specific pricing: different prices on the same products to different customers being triggered by the customer's frequent shopper card at the point of sale.

Quantity limits? Associated with customer group or true customer specific pricing are quantity limits, or minimum purchases. For example, is it possible to sell a product to "gold" customers with no limits or minimum purchase, while permitting "silver" customers a limit of three purchases with no minimum purchase, and at the same time letting "bronze" customers buy only one of the items with a minimum $10 purchase? Quantity limits and minimum purchases are simply another form of pricing. Will the POS allow differentiating between customers in these areas?

Random weight capability? Another area related to the POS that becomes important, especially in the supermarket channel, is that of random weight products. Can the POS accept items on discount, with a frequent shopper card, that are sold by weight? Again, some of the older systems in use cannot accommodate this; the newer technologies can. In any retail business where some portion of the goods being sold are sold by weight, the ability to include these products in the retailer's frequent shopper program is very important.

Let's digress slightly while addressing random weight frequent shopper products. This really is a two-part issue. One part is the POS system being able to handle random weight products being sold at two prices: regular price and the frequent shopper price. The next issue is how to communicate the price to the customer. Retailers have typically had to label the random weight package with the regular price, and attempt to inform the customers that their frequent shopper discount would take effect when they check out. Though retailers have had success operating this way, many customers would prefer to see the package marked with their frequent shopper price.

A few of the leading scale manufacturers, such as Hobart, have addressed this concern very capably. Their scale systems will support frequent shopper programs with labels that state the regular price per pound, the package weight, and the regular package price, as well as the frequent shopper price per pound and the frequent shopper package price.

How are discounts calculated? Can the POS calculate different dollar-off amounts or percent-off amounts to different customer groups or specific customers on the same items? These things become important when building promotions to different customers or customer groups. Perhaps you want to give one customer a percentage off, but a different customer, a dollar-off amount.

Points program capability? Will the POS support a points program? Most will support a basic points program where, for example, a customer earns one point for each dollar spent. More advanced programs prefer to differentiate on points also. The retailer offers the customer bonus points for purchasing certain items, with specific customers or customer groups being able to accumulate points faster.

Reporting capabilities? Is the POS able to track item movement and markdown expense by customer group? In addition, all stores with scanning do some kind of price verification, making sure the price charged by the computer matches the sign or the shelf tag. Will the POS allow verification by customer group on the sales floor? For example, can it verify an item that is sold at three different prices (regular price, sale price with card, and "gold" customer price)?

Cashier card activity? Integrity of the data is essential for the customer specific retail enterprise. Can the POS system monitor cashier card activity to make sure that no abuse is occurring? For example, can it detect a cashier who is using his or her own card to give customers discounts?

Customer look-up capability? Sooner or later, a customer will come through the checkout line who has legitimately forgotten his or her card. Can the POS system look up the customer's card number? Some systems can look up a customer by name or telephone number.

The POS system can also be an important customer communication vehicle, which will be further discussed in Section Four. Here are some of the ways the latest technology can assist with customer communication.

Customer monitor / cashier monitor. Some systems offer a dual monitor capability. The cashier's monitor displays the information needed for the transaction, as well as the customer's name, so the cashier can personalize the transaction. The customer monitor can show a running sub-total of the order, as well as greeting the customer by name when the customer's card is scanned. In addition, space on the monitor is devoted to marketing messages, which can include customer group specific messaging.

Receipt printer. Most of the newer systems use a thermal printer, which allows the use of graphics on the receipt. Minimally, the retailer should print the total of the cardholder's savings in that transaction, or his or her new points total. Ideally, the POS should support customer group specific or individual customer specific messaging capabilities on the bottom of the receipt. For example, the POS should be able to print out several specials the customer can receive on his or her next shopping visit.

Database Systems

Perhaps the most important building block is the database system used to store and analyze the great amounts of detailed customer information gathered through a retail frequent shopper program. The capabilities and flexibility of the database will determine current and future marketing and management efforts.

As in the technology industry as a whole, there is a great deal of change occurring in this area. The ideal solution is still being sought, but there are several choices that present themselves.

RMS's MarketEXPERT (203.925.9039) is perhaps the most established of the frequent shopper database systems. It is in use by retailers of all sizes throughout North and South America, as well as by a number of retailers in

Europe. Catalina Coupon (727.579.5000) has expanded into the database side of the business, capturing transaction level data through their existing coupon system, and then making this information available to the retailers. XiNETix (954.969.3000) continues to offer outstanding capabilities to design and run different promotions, all delivered through their in-lane printers.

SASI (Store Automated Systems, Inc.) (215.785.4329) became a contender in the frequent shopper area by being one of the first POS vendors to offer a system capable of supporting customer group and true customer specific pricing. SASI now has branched off into the database side of the business with their Allegiance product. They have been very aggressive in tying together all the technologies needed by retailers to support customer specific retailing: the database, kiosks to communicate one-to-one with customers, and the POS to electronically deliver customer specific offers.

Both RMS and SASI are developing data modeling and predictive analysis capabilities. These systems will predict, with good levels of accuracy, customers at risk of defecting as well as those with the most potential to respond to a specific offer. This is an exciting new breakthrough, using expert data systems to sort through the massive amounts of data in retailer databases, to help us more efficiently target our efforts.

We are seeing a great deal of interest, especially on the part of larger companies practicing product category management, in overlaying product information with customer information. This is evolving into a matrix structure with product category information being overlaid with customer category information. This concept will be addressed much more completely in Chapter 11, but when evaluating database solutions, the retailer should give thought to how easily this type of data interaction can be accomplished.

The ability to segment customers based on a great variety of criteria is critical to customer specific retailing. Certainly, the attributes of spending, frequency, and recency of shopping are mainstays. Will the database you are considering allow you to segment customers based on their purchasing habits? Many retailers will ask on their card applications if the customer has a dog (with the intent of sending the customer offers on dog food). Would it not be easier to simply go into the database and see which customers are regular buyers of dog food? Maybe Mr. Smith did not have a dog when he signed up for the card, but adopted a dog a few months later. A record of actual shopping behavior is priceless.

What are the reporting capabilities of the database? Are you limited to whatever stock reports come with the package, or can you tailor the reports to your needs? Does it have some kind of report writer functionality so that you can design reports as you need them? Can you export your data to another platform or program for further analysis?

Is it possible to export limited information from the database to store level or to your customer service department? Many retailers have found it helpful for their store managers or service representatives to have access to a portion of the database to determine what type of customer they are speaking with. For example, is the customer at the "gold" or "bronze" level? They find it helpful to have such information when presented with a customer service situation.

How much data can you maintain on-line? It is critical to have at least 15 months of transaction-level data on-line for analysis purposes. This allows a retailer to do quarter-to-quarter, year-on-year comparisons when looking at customer defection rates, same household purchasing trends, etc. The more data, the better.

Should retailers use a service bureau or handle their data in-house? There are successful applications of each of these primary methods for maintaining and using data. There is no right or wrong with regard to this choice; it is a function of management philosophy, and possibly, cost. Questions to consider with a service bureau have to do with how timely and rapidly you can get your management reports. Are you limited to standard reports, or can you execute custom queries on the data? Do you have access to the data anytime, or only periodically?

An entire book could be written about database capabilities related to retail frequent shopper programs. Rather than do this here, and because it would be out-of-date before the book could be published, let me distill the thoughts related to this area to this: until recently, these database systems were developed as *marketing tools.* As retailers have advanced their efforts, these systems are now being used as *management tools.* Make sure that the database system you choose can process the information you need to support your efforts and decision making in all areas of your business, not just marketing.

In the customer specific retail enterprise, information is the foundation for all that happens. As the tools continue to develop, we may see systems that are put in place similar to the one shown in Figure 3-1. There must be a central repository of all detailed customer and product information. This then supports efforts in merchandising, operations, customer communications and support, marketing initiatives, and, most importantly, the financial reporting. For this information to be maximally utilized, all the systems must "balance," that is, they must tie out at the end of the day.

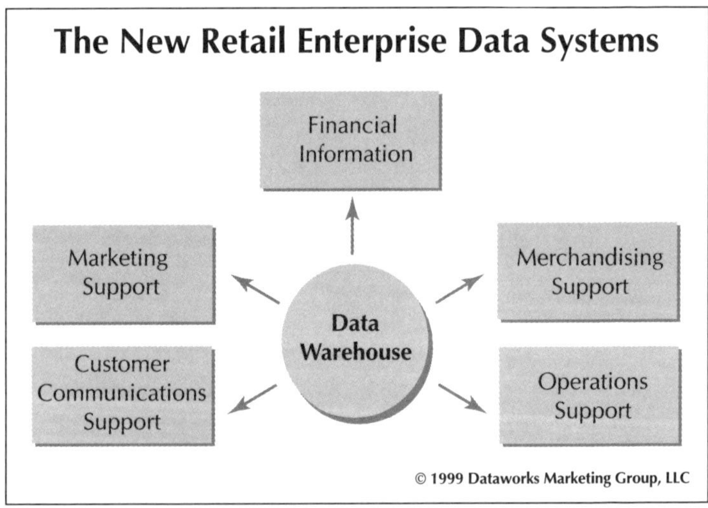

Figure 3-1

Too often in today's retail organizations, product information resides separately from marketing information; and financial information has no direct tie to either of them. We see extensive product category management initiatives in place in larger retailers, but they are not integrated with the company's profit and loss statements or balance sheet. The new retail enterprise looks to close the loop, integrating all product and customer information with the financial reporting, to maximize its potential. It is only when we measure something that we can truly begin to manage it.

Networks

It is not enough to capture the detailed customer information at the point of sale. It must be moved to the database to be of any use. In any retail operation having more than two locations, this means some type of computer network communication.

The bar in this area is being raised very quickly. Just a couple of years ago, it was rare for a multi-store retailer to have a real time, on-line network in place among their stores. Today, more and more retailers, both large and small, have, or are putting in place, this capability.

Obviously, the customer information must be moved from the POS to the database; but just as importantly, information must flow from the database to the store to be effective. To maximize the effectiveness of all this information, many retailers are finding it necessary to provide some information back to their store level personnel; having some type of communication network in place facilitates this.

Perhaps more importantly, retailers need to relay back to customers information relative to their status on different marketing programs. For example, customers of Albert Heijn, a Netherlands based supermarket chain, can scan their cards at a kiosk near the entrance of any of their stores to learn their current points balances. This technology is supported by a state-of-the-art on-line, real time, computer network.

Increasingly, customer communication is becoming electronically based. As such, communication tools like web sites, and interactive voice response (IVR) systems, in addition to kiosks, are becoming an important part of a company's network.

Frequent Shopper Cards

The last building block is the frequent shopper cards themselves. The choices here are many.

Card or key tag? The early retailers used a wallet-style card as their frequent shopper card, modeling their programs after credit card companies or airline frequent flier cards. Over the past several years, we have seen key tags with a bar code or magnetic stripe on the back become very popular. Some feel the key tags are more convenient for customers than a card.

Bar code or magnetic stripe? Bar coded cards or key tags are substantially less expensive than magnetic stripes.

Magnetic stripe cards or key tags are necessary, though, for any type of financial services to be added to the card. To date, we still are not seeing great acceptance and use of "smart cards." While some retailers are using them in Europe, the technology seems to be too expensive for use in frequent shopper programs at the present time. As the technology continues to improve, and the cost of these cards containing a computer chip continues to decline, they will most likely play an important role in customer specific retailing.

Individual cards or family identification? This is an important question that retailers must ask themselves before launching a program. Will you issue individual cards to individual family members, each with a unique number, or will you issue a group of cards, sometimes called a family pack, to the customer? Family packs, typically consisting of one or two wallet cards and two key tags, all with the same frequent shopper number, are the most cost-effective. When the customer signs up, he or she is given the family pack with the suggestion to give a card or key tag to his or her spouse and any other family member who may shop.

Other retailers give separate cards or key tags to individual customers. For example, a customer who signs up will be given a key tag and asked if his or her spouse would like one. Each individual has his or her own specific frequent shopper number, but all family members are linked together in the database to create a household.

An important question when looking down the road to true customer specific marketing is: do you want to

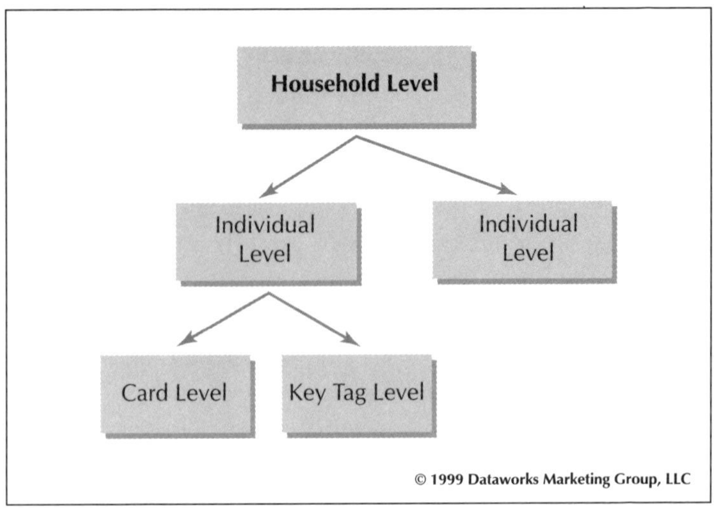

Figure 3-2

market by household level or by individual customer level? For example, John and Joanie are a family, and each does some shopping. Marketing at the household level, both would receive the same set of offers. At an individual level, Joanie would receive offers for the types of products she likes to buy, while John would receive offers relative to his preferences, as expressed in his past purchasing behavior.

This is an important decision, to which a retailer should give a great deal of thought prior to launching a program. While there is much that can be accomplished with household level data, eventually we may find that marketing individually to our customers, even those within the same household, offers a strong payback. Retailers who issued family pack cards will then be faced with the challenge of having to re-issue individual cards to their customer base, an expensive process and one that can irritate customers.

It may well be that technology will answer the question of what is best regarding household level or individual level information gathering and marketing. One of the largest point-of-sale providers is building into its newest systems the capability to handle bio-metric identification, such as fingerprints or a thumb scan. One of the United State's largest retailers is experimenting with the use of bio-metric identification tied to its check cashing approval system and eventually to its frequent shopper program. As technology progresses, it is very likely some form of bio-metric identification will arise to supplant the plastic cards and key tags typical today.

Perhaps household level versus individual level data should be thought of this way: management reporting and reward programs are done at the household level. True one-to-one marketing will require individual level information capabilities.

Time given to internal discussions relative to the long-term goals and aspirations of the retailer about to launch a frequent shopper program is time well-spent. Too many companies simply jump in, almost assembling their card programs on the fly, and do not take the time to think through and plan their long term strategies.

For the new retail enterprise, technology and information systems are strategic weapons.

Building the Foundation

Chapter 4: Creating the Blueprint

As with any building project, it is necessary to start with a plan — a blueprint. And, just as when embarking on the construction of an important building, the architect must be chosen with care. Top management of the retailer must understand and have a comprehensive view of all that must happen to build the new retail enterprise. Without commitment and understanding from top management, the new building is destined to fail.

When the basic strategy and incentive scheme has been decided on, and the necessary hardware and software systems assembled, it is time to develop the implementation plan.

As previously noted, the customer specific retail enterprise requires vast amounts of information: upwards of 80% of all sales and 60% of total transactions. The world record for attaining these rates is 10 days from launch!

This record is shared by three supermarket companies: an independent, a regional chain, and a large chain with over 200 stores! This serves to illustrate an important point: with proper planning and good execution, any retailer can very quickly establish a frequent shopper program and begin capturing massive amounts of detailed customer information.

Along with top management, the entire management team of the enterprise must be educated in this new way of practicing retail. This is an ongoing process. Typically, we see retailers of all sizes move through an evolution in their thinking and acceptance of this area. Initially, retailers may realize intellectually that all their customers are not equal — for example, that the top 30% of their customers are supplying them with 75% of the annual volume. While they intellectually accept this concept, there is some internal doubt as to whether this truly applies to their unique stores. Once a program is launched and data gathered, these retailers do indeed see that they are no different; all their customers are not equal.

As they move into acceptance that all their customers are not equal, management typically develops a willingness to experiment with differentiation between customers. Done properly, this differentiation — usually accomplished through some type of spend and reward program — generates a profitable return on investment. As this occurs, actual understanding and real, emotional commitment to card based retailing begins to take place.

A very important element of building a strong foundation for customer specific retailing is building a *card culture*. By this, I mean that everyone within the organization must be knowledgeable and supportive of the retailer's card program. Without a strong card culture, retailers will have a very difficult time building a solid enough foundation for their future efforts.

This is a new way to go to market. It means letting go of some of the old ways, and adopting new marketing methods and uses of information. The gathering, understanding, and use of customer information must become core to the company.

Without doubt, building this card culture must begin at the top. The owner or president, and the top management team, must be totally committed to developing and operating a frequent shopper card program. As we look around the world, we see that those retailers who are most successful with their programs are characterized by a top management team that is committed to gathering, understanding, and using customer information, and that drives this throughout their organization. Conversely, those retailers having only moderate success, or worse, are characterized by a top management team that does not get it; they view a card program as simply another marketing or promotional program. They do not grasp and understand the strategic implications of having and using detailed customer information.

For one year prior to launching a frequent shopper program, the president of a large, regional supermarket chain attended a weekly meeting, one-to-two hours long, dedicated to planning the launch of his company's program. That is commitment. This company went on to launch their program very successfully; they were identifying more than 80% of sales through their card within two weeks of launch. Within the first few months they also experienced substantial sales and profit gains.

At a different regional chain, the story was quite the opposite. This supermarket retailer launched its frequent shopper card with a blizzard of advertising. Upon visiting the stores, it was apparent that their execution was lacking. They were issuing two cards to customers, one with check cashing privileges, one without. Their store personnel were poorly trained, and cashiers did not know which card to issue or how to do it. I asked for a card when purchasing a few items and the cashier simply gave me a card — without asking me to fill out an application! Needless to say, this program was a failure; the company withdrew its card program within a year of launch.

The card culture must extend beyond top management to include everyone in the company. The people on the front lines, a retailer's cashiers and other store-level people, can make or break a program. Many retailers have meetings at store level with their entire work force announcing their upcoming programs, and educating the employees as to what their card program is all about and its goals.

Some time ago, I spent a day with a regional supermarket chain that had a card program in place for a little over a year's time. The chain had begun running different marketing programs rewarding customers' spending. At the same time, the retailer had serious systems problems and was losing great amounts of data, thus not capturing shoppers' spending accurately. The situation became so bad that I overheard cashiers telling customers to please not use their frequent shopper cards, because they never worked right and were a real headache!

Leading retailers realize that building this card culture must begin at the top, and extend outside the organization to customers. Kevin Doris, President of Gerland's Food Fair in Houston, Texas, keeps a supply of five-minute phone cards in his pocket. Whenever he is out somewhere and sees a customer with a Gerland's key tag, he introduces himself and presents the customer with a free phone card!

Leading companies include their store-level personnel in their results as much as possible. For example, clients we work with post the weekly identification rates (sales and transactions done through the card) at store level in the employee lounge. Some retailers run different types of reward programs solely for their associate households. The more "buy-in" by associates, the better.

For purposes of discussion, we will define three areas that need to be addressed in assembling an implementation plan.

Systems

By systems, we mean the computer systems necessary to capture and compile detailed customer information and other related procedures. This includes the POS systems and the database package.

One of the best practices we have seen evolve is retailers launching their programs first with their associates, and then, after a period of up to three months, publicly launching their program for customers. This practice gets the retailer two important things: 1) it allows the retailer to test all the hardware and software systems to insure everything is working properly; and 2) it allows the retailer to reward their associates, thus getting them on board.

It is not uncommon, especially in larger retailers, for problems to turn up when first bringing a system online. For this reason, the above practice is an ideal way of "burning in" a system without risking customer disillusionment.

Another related systems issue involves the synchronization of UPC files and department structures in multi-store enterprises. It is not uncommon for PLU #100 to represent one item in one store, while the same PLU number represents a different, unrelated product in another store. This becomes important when the information is transferred back to the database.

Lisa Piron, of DataWorks Marketing Group, expresses concern about a related area. "I can't emphasize enough the importance of customers being able to have faith in the data being reported back to them. Retailers running reward programs tied to customer spending must have accurate data files. Many customers save their receipts; the retailer's total for the reward program had better match the customer's receipts, or there's a problem."

Operations

First, an accounting decision must be made. If requiring the card for price discounts, retailers must choose whether to track this markdown expense in their bookkeeping. This normally entails recording sales at regular price, thus expanding the gross margin, and then expensing the cost of the markdown.

Another decision must be made relative to the start-up expenses related to the program. Should they be expensed or capitalized?

Card applications should be brief and easy for the customer to complete. We suggest asking for only the basic information: name, address, telephone number, number of people in household, and if the customer would like any additional cards for other household members. Birthday information is sometimes requested, but not commonly given.

A related area is how the customer data will be entered into the database. This can be done in-house; many times retailers hire temporary staff to accomplish this. An alternative is to outsource the data entry to an outside firm. Some companies, such as Moore, will provide the applications, cards, and data entry as a single service. If OCR (optical character recognition) scanning is used to enter the data, we suggest doing a test to determine error rates before proceeding. Without accurate data at this stage, the retailer will be destined for headaches later.

Retailers typically have meetings with their associates at store level prior to launch. This is a good opportunity to get a card into each of your associate's hands. A nice touch is to do the data entry from their personnel information, thereby saving the associate from having to complete any paperwork.

When Leevers (Colorado) launched their card program, management held meetings with all store-level people to announce and explain the program and answer any questions. John Leevers, at the time responsible for human resources, put together an excellent training package, including commonly asked questions and answers, to prep his people for responding to customers. In addition, the store offered their employees special pricing on a dozen or so items each week for several weeks prior to launch. This allowed Leevers to test their systems, as well as reward their people with extra savings, thus helping to bring the employees on board with the program.

Glen's Markets, a supermarket chain located in Gaylord, Michigan, also did an outstanding job of getting their people involved. The chain took over a school auditorium for a day and held a meeting of all management-level people. The owner and other key people responsible for developing the card program delivered presentations about what the company was doing and why. Glen's Markets developed an excellent brochure for all employees, explaining what the Glen's Markets Valued Customer Card program was all about, and addressing commonly asked questions. In addition, Glen's Markets ran a card based sweepstakes open only to employees — with a new car as the grand prize.

Launch Marketing Strategy

The first question that must be addressed in this area is whether you want your to launch to be fast or slow. By that, I mean whether you wish to attain the 80%-plus identification of total sales quickly — in a matter of days — or to proceed slowly and attain it within months?

Our strong suggestion is that a retailer progress to this level very quickly and aggressively. The sooner you start capturing a high level of customer information, the sooner you can begin using it to improve your profitability. It is also important to send a very clear message to your customers. That message must be that you believe in your frequent shopper program, and that it can deliver real value to your customers. Retailers who equivocate, risk customer acceptance of their card at the time of launch, a time when top management is very attuned to customer comments, especially negative ones!

Retailers tying their card to their markdown typically move 50% of their advertised specials onto the card the first week of their program, 75% in the third week, and 100% by the fourth week. Chris Leevers, head of card marketing for Leevers Supermarkets, commented after the launch of their first store that he would have moved to 100% of all markdown on the card even more quickly!

Doing this successfully — and it has been done successfully by a number of retailers now — requires very good planning and strong execution at store level.

One of the good practices we have seen develop is that of the retailers putting their card application into their newspaper ads when launching. The customer is then able to complete the application at home. This saves time and confusion in the store — the customer simply stops by the sign-up table or service desk to receive his or her card. Many retailers have used this practice to good advantage.

Chuck McNett, Director of Marketing for Niemann Foods, executed what is perhaps a textbook launch of their Max Saver card during the summer of 1997. Newspaper ads, including a card application, signaled the launch of their frequent shopper card.

Customers arriving at their stores were greeted with banners hung outside promoting their card. Upon entering the store, customers were greeted with a special sign-up table, staffed by specially trained store-level employees, where they could complete an application, receive their Max saver card and key tag on-the-spot, and learn all about the benefits the new card offered.

Walking through the store, customers were met in each aisle by banners and other signs, all promoting the Max card. Niemann even put a kiosk in each store, complete with a television playing a recorded message explaining the benefits of getting and using the new frequent shopper card.

All of Niemanns' price reductions were also moved very aggressively onto the Max Saver card. In less than one month, 100% of the price reductions required the use of their frequent shopper card. This also resulted in a more streamlined look in their signage around the store. Whereas before the card launch there were a number of different sign packages used to support different merchandising programs, at card launch there was only one: the Max Saver card.

Niemann began a sweepstakes tied to the frequent shopper card at the time of launch. Each time customers used their card they received one entry into a sweepstakes offering a number of different prizes. The grand prize was a trip to Disney World.

Within several months of launch, Niemann ran their first free Thanksgiving turkey program. Niemann did an excellent job of planning ahead of time the different card based marketing initiatives that would be brought out during the first year. The idea was to, on a regular basis, layer in additional values and incentives for customer card use.

The results? Niemann was identifying more than 90% of total sales within the first two weeks of launch. Niemann has continued to sustain this level of information gathering since then.

How will you handle customers, especially at the time of launch, who do not have a card and yet still request the discounts? Some stores use a manager's card at the front end, which can be swiped for customers who do not yet have their cards. This is viable at the time of launch but must be taken away within the first week or two, lest it develop bad habits on the part of customers. They will come to think they don't need their cards when shopping!

A related area that should be covered in associate training is how you wish your cashiers to handle the "no card, no discount" rule when dealing with customers? There should be some procedure developed to deal with this eventuality.

The privacy issue needs to be addressed from day one of a frequent shopper program. Leading retailers develop policies and procedures concerning the internal and external use of their detailed customer information. These companies are very aware of the trust and relationship they have with their customers. Typically, they develop very strong policies telling their customers that the information gathered will remain confidential to the retailer, and will never be sold or released to any outside company.

We recommend that retailers take a very proactive approach to the privacy issue. Be up front with customers regarding the information you are gathering; customers realize what you are doing.

Initially, the retailer does not have any meaningful data to really look at and analyze. For the first few weeks, indeed months, we strongly recommend that retailers concentrate on monitoring their identification rates (what percentage of their total sales and transactions are being done with their frequent shopper cards). These totals should be viewed by store, by weekly total; there will be fluctuations when looked at by daily totals. If using some type of manager's card, remember to block this card so that it does not influence the reports you are viewing.

There are several lessons to take away from this section. The everyday incentive scheme must be cost-effective and yet provide strong encouragement for our customers to obtain and use their cards, so that we are able to gather high levels of information. Successful card marketers realize that they cannot simply layer more costs onto their existing operations to support their card programs. These companies look to reduce expenses in their advertising and marketing areas in order to redirect money to support their incentive plans, sweepstakes, and other reward programs.

Section 3: Building the New Enterprise Structure

It is frightening to see the lack of quality information some retailers have regarding their businesses. Sometimes it is worse among larger companies than small. Some retailers capitalize their promotional expenses, while others use suspense accounts for their trade monies, which are then pulled into their financial statements when needed to "make their numbers." Other retailers do not know what their markdown expenditures are, or what gross profit margin they are essentially buying from their wholesaler or supplier. They have, in effect, built their houses of straw.

Other retailers have built a more elaborate structure using their product information. While we cannot fault these companies — after all, product based measures were the only thing available until recently — their structures can be likened to a house of sticks. While more secure than

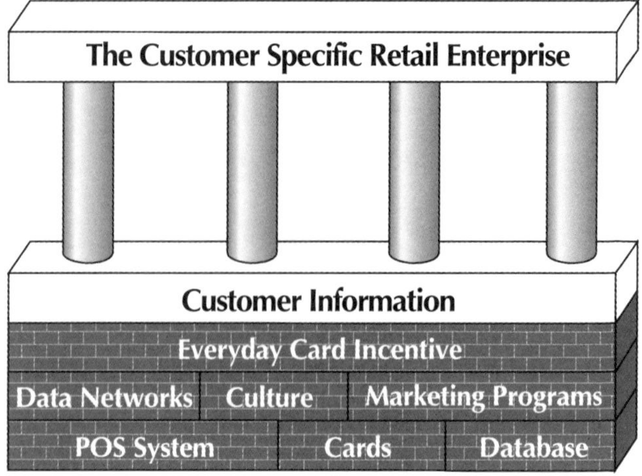

straw, building their companies based only on product information has left them vulnerable to new forms of competition. Having invested heavily in a product based company infrastructure, they are slow to adopt the new measures offered by detailed customer information.

I was speaking at a conference where I shared the platform with a representative from a company that packages manufacturer offers for retailers in the supermarket industry. I was shocked when, during the course of our conversation backstage he told me, "Too many retailers are lazy; they basically want to turn over their businesses to the manufacturers, sit back and collect their money." While a strong statement, it is nonetheless accurate in too many cases.

The customer specific retailer has built a house of stone, adding customer based measures to the product measures available previously. By now being able to see and measure the shopping behavior of their customers, customer specific retailers have built a more solid enterprise, one better able to withstand changes in the industry and from competitors.

The customer specific retailer now has control over their entire operation. By integrating customer information into their operations, they are able to solidify their customer base and build a stronger business.

Building the New Enterprise Structure

Chapter 5: Customer Category Management

As we have seen in Brian Woolf's work, and in other evidence presented earlier in this book, our customers are not all equal to us in economic value. Our higher-spending customers are more profitable to us than our lower-spending customers or the cherry pickers. All sales are not equal. Because of this, we now need a new way to view our businesses.

Because we are now speaking of differences *within* our customer base, we need to look beneath the surface of our top line of sales. In somewhat humorous terms, think of this as being akin to the example shown in Figure 5-1. Every retailer has a certain number of high-spending customers, the "high-spending whales" in this example. All retailers have convenience customers, the "convenience cod." There are many secondary customers in every retailer's customer base, customers who split their shopping between several competing stores; let's call them the "secondary starfish." And every retailer who does any type of price promotion has what we will call the "scavenger sharks."

Figure 5-1

What I am trying to stress with this example is that: all retailers must now know what types of customers they have, how many they have of each of them, and whether their numbers are increasing or decreasing. As change in the composition of the customer base occurs, it directly correlates with the profit margins of the retailer, due to the differences in customer group profitability. This is all happening beneath the surface of our total sales.

It is no longer enough for retailers to simply measure and manage their top line sales.

To effectively measure these groups, and to record the changes over time, we need a scorecard. That scorecard is customer category management. Very simply, customer category management is the segmentation of the customer base by economics, not by demographics.

Economics and finance are what drive any business; therefore, we must view our customer bases along these lines.

There is a very real and important difference between customer category management as it is presented here, and the decile reports that are produced by many of the database products being used by retailers to support their frequent shopper efforts. A decile report simply divides the data into 10 groups, each representing a 10% segment of the total. For example, the sample report shown in Figure 5-2 divides the customer base into 10 groups, each representing 10% of the total customers by their sales. As you can see in this sample report, the spending range of each decile is stated, along with the number of customers in each decile, their frequency of shopping, the total sales of the customers in each decile, and the average household spending per week.

Decile Spending Report — 4 Week Period / Year 1

Decile	Decile Spending Range Min.	Max.	No. of HH	Frequency Trans./Wk.	Sales $	Average $ per HH/Wk.
10	$195.38	$1,112.88	907	2.71	$294,013.77	$81.04
9	156.01	187.35	902	1.96	168,583.11	46.72
8	116.09	155.97	902	1.59	121,943.07	33.80
7	86.32	116.07	902	1.37	90,473.83	25.08
6	63.73	86.31	902	1.2	67,539.66	18.72
5	45.42	63.72	902	1.03	48,614.18	13.47
4	31.34	45.41	902	0.82	34,712.97	9.62
3	20.10	31.30	902	0.68	23,017.95	6.38
2	10.51	20.07	902	0.5	13,785.18	3.82
1	0.09	10.49	902	0.37	5,390.85	1.49

* Data from "Berkeley" Markets.

Figure 5-2

A decile report is an easy way to begin to understand the data. Using decile reports, there is always a top 10% or a bottom 30%, but their sales can be dramatically different over time.

Figure 5-3 shows two decile reports from the same retailer. Each report represents a four-week period of time, but the same four-week period from different years. Look at how the spending levels in each decile have changed.

Decile Spending Report — 4 Week Period / Year 1

Decile	Decile Spending Range Min.	Max.	No. of HH	Frequency Trans./Wk.	Sales $	Average $ per HH/Wk.
10	$195.38	$1,112.88	907	2.71	$294,013.77	$81.04
9	156.01	187.35	902	1.96	168,583.11	46.72
8	116.09	155.97	902	1.59	121,943.07	33.80
7	86.32	116.07	902	1.37	90,473.83	25.08
6	63.73	86.31	902	1.2	67,539.66	18.72
5	45.42	63.72	902	1.03	48,614.18	13.47
4	31.34	45.41	902	0.82	34,712.97	9.62
3	20.10	31.30	902	0.68	23,017.95	6.38
2	10.51	20.07	902	0.5	13,785.18	3.82
1	0.09	10.49	902	0.37	5,390.85	1.49

Decile Spending Report — 4 Week Period / Year 3

Decile	Decile Spending Range Min.	Max.	No. of HH	Frequency Trans./Wk.	Sales $	Average $ per HH/Wk.
10	$332.26	$1,211.32	938	4.11	$437,811.43	$116.69
9	216.94	332.01	942	2.76	253,255.35	67.21
8	141.43	216.83	942	2.14	166,068.71	44.07
7	98.08	141.35	942	1.64	110,996.31	29.46
6	69.24	98.07	942	1.27	78,481.07	20.83
5	47.42	69.20	942	1.02	54,247.91	14.40
4	30.65	47.40	942	0.77	36,186.40	9.61
3	18.78	30.58	942	0.58	22,916.45	6.08
2	9.52	18.77	942	0.43	13,219.36	3.50
1	—	9.51	942	0.34	4,761.05	1.26

* Data from "Berkeley" Markets.

Figure 5-3

Let me provide an example drawn from these sample reports. In Year 1, a customer household spending $50 a week average ($200 in four weeks) was a decile 10 customer, the best. Over time, the retailer begins to actively change customer spending in their store with some success. By Year 3, the same customer, still spending $50 a week average ($200 in four weeks), is now a decile 8 customer — good, but no longer the best. This particular customer has not changed his or her behavior. He or she has maintained the same spending level, but the retailer has been able to increase other customers' spending, thereby raising the bar for a decile 10 customer, as shown in Figure 5-4.

The problem that this example serves to illustrate, lies in how retailers define and recognize their best customers. Many retailers offer rewards only to their top 10% or top 30% of customers. These rewards may be special prices, free products, newsletters, etc. While this is logical think-

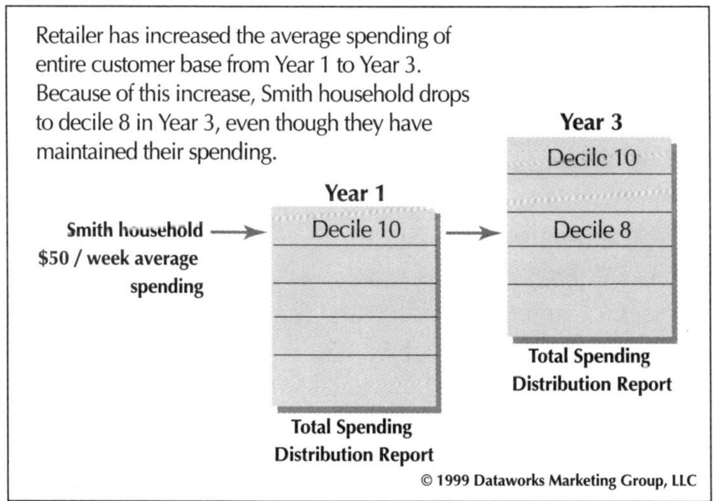

Figure 5-4

ing — take care of your best customers — is it right to essentially downgrade customers who have maintained their spending with you over time, as in our example?

Yet another way that retailers are segmenting their customers is by using an R-F-S segmentation method. RFS stands for Recency, Frequency, and Spending (also sometimes referred to as Money as in RFM analysis). This database marketing approach originated in the direct mail industry and has been carried over to the retail industry.

Using this method, retailers first rank their customers by spending, much as in a decile report. They may use deciles, quintiles, quartiles, or any other grouping. They then rank their customers based upon recency of shopping using the same number of segments. Lastly, the retailer segments their customer base by shopping frequency. When finished, the retailer or analyst has a table that looks something like the one following.

	Spending	Recency	Frequency
Top 30% of customers	S1	R1	F1
Middle 40% of customers	S2	R2	F2
Bottom 30% of customers	S3	R3	F3

Next, the retailer combines these different segments into a matrix. Because we have three factors, each having three different customer segments, the matrix will have 27 (3^3) combinations, such as R1 F1 S1, or R2 F1 S3, and so on.

Marketers using this segmentation tool then use it to drive their marketing efforts. Marketers have found that customers in the top ranking of any of the three variables are most likely to respond to an offer, to shop again with that company. There are then other combinations of segments possible; different marketers have their own opinions about the value of these other segments and the value of marketing to the people within them.

While the value of this has been proven in the direct mail industry, its application in the retail industry depends upon the goals of the retailer. Traditional database marketing entails drilling down into the data, creating smaller and smaller segments while trying to increase the redemption rate of offers, thus increasing the return on investment for the marketing effort. In customer specific retailing, we leapfrog this entire process, moving directly to looking at each individual customer's shopping behavior. The marketing message for each individual customer is then created from the customer's shopping history.

A decile analysis or RFS segmentation is simply a marketing tool, constrained by its inherent limitations of being a moving target, the numbers changing each time the analysis is done. Customer category management is first and foremost a management tool, one that can additionally be used for marketing purposes. For data to be used as a measurement tool over time, it must have some kind of baseline to which it can be compared. This is the power of customer category management.

Customer category management provides us with the scorecard for establishing the composition of our customer base, and for measuring changes in this composition over time. It also provides the framework for evaluating our marketing and operational decisions in new ways. It is now possible, using customer category management (CCM), to begin matching marketing expenditures to the different revenue streams offered by different customer groups. Think back to the reward pyramids shown in Chapter 1. CCM provides the measurement system for aligning the marketing rewards (markdown, advertising, etc.) with the different customer groups.

Figure 5-5 represents a very simplified customer category management report. In this example, we are dividing up the total sales over five different customer categories. The "whale" category represents those customers averaging purchases of more than $100 a week; the "starfish" category consists of customers with average purchases of between $50 and $100 a week, and so on. We can now see the different revenue streams offered by our different

Customer Category Management Report — 12 Week Report

Average SPW	Customer Category	Sales $	Sales as % of total	Households	HH's as % of Total	Average HH $/wk	Frequency of Shopping (visits/week)
	Unidentified	$132,000	10%	?	?	?	
<$24.99	Sharks	312,000	23%	3980	73.7%	$ 6.53	0.625
$25-$49.99	Cod	288,000	22%	772	14.3%	31.09	1.4
$50-$99.99	Starfish	360,000	27%	556	10.3%	53.96	2.3
$100 +	Whales	240,000	18%	92	1.7%	217.39	3.1
	TOTAL	***$1,332,000***	100%	5400	100%	$ 20.56	

This report shows total sales (for a period: week, month, quarter, etc.) by customer category. We can now see what percent of total sales each customer category generates. We can also report the number of households in each customer category and their average household spending per week (in this example, we are using 12 weeks of data). We can now also view the frequency of shopping by our different customers by category.

Figure 5-5

customers, as well as the number of customer households in each category.

The numbers used in reports 5-5 and 5-6 were created with data from a number of different retailers. While the sales numbers do not reflect any particular store(s), the ratios between customer categories, such as in percent of total sales, households, and frequency are based upon actual retailer numbers.

In addition, just as there are differences among customers with regard to their purchases, there are accompanying differences relative to their profitability. Some of the more advanced retailers, with the necessary information systems, are able to view their profitability by customer category. As can be seen from the example in Figure 5-6, the higher-spending customers are the most profitable. In this example, we are using simplified gross profit margin numbers for purposes of illustration. These numbers do, however, have some basis in fact. One large North American supermarket chain did indeed find almost a 10% differential in the gross profit margins offered by its highest-spending customers and its lowest-spending customers.

Again, the sales numbers used in report 5-6 represent no particular retailer. The ratios between customer categories are reflective of certain retailers' experience.

The changes shown in report 5-6 between Year 1 and Year 3 are indicative of the change in a retailer's customer base. The increase in gross margin in the "starfish" and "whale" categories come about as the retailer is able

Customer Category Management Report — Year 1

Average SPW	Customer Category	Sales $	Sales as % of total	Households	HH's as % of total	Gross Margin %	Gross Margin $
	Unidentified	$ 132,000	10%	?	?	20%	$ 26,400
<$24.99	Sharks	331,000	25%	3980	73.7%	15%	49,650
$25-$49.99	Cod	313,000	23%	772	14.3%	18%	56,340
$50-$99.99	Starfish	433,000	33%	556	10.3%	22%	95,260
$100 +	Whales	123,000	9%	92	1.7%	25%	30,750
	TOTAL	***$1,332,000***	100%	5400	100%	***19.40%***	***$258,400***

Customer Category Management Report — Year 3

Average SPW	Customer Category	Sales $	Sales as % of total	Households	HH's as % of total	Gross Margin %	Gross Margin $
	Unidentified	$ 132,000	10%	?	?	20%	$ 26,400
<$24.99	Sharks	272,000	20%	3850	71.3%	15%	40,800
$25-$49.99	Cod	276,000	21%	772	14.3%	18%	49,680
$50-$99.99	Starfish	418,000	31%	594	11.0%	23%	96,140
$100 +	Whales	234,000	18%	184	3.4%	26%	60,840
	TOTAL	***$1,332,000***	100%	5400	100%	***20.56%***	***$273,860***

SPW = Spending Per Week

For purposes of this report we are using assumed gross profit margins of each customer category as are stated. These do indeed have some basis in fact; one large supermarket chain found a 10% differential in margins between its lowest- and highest-spending customers. Some retailers are very near to reporting profitability by customer, built from the item level up.

This report is simply illustrating the change in total company profitability possible by changing the composition of the customer base; for example, increasing the number of Gold customers from 1.7% to 3.4% of total customers, and increasing their proportion to total sales from 9% to 18%, all under the surface of level total sales volume. Experience has shown that as higher-spending customers increase their spending, their gross profit margin also increases as they purchase more items at full price and more higher-margin perishable products.

Figure 5-6

to encourage these customers to spend more. As they increase spending, these customers are purchasing more products at full price and more higher-margin perishables, thus effecting an increase in their profitability to the retailer.

As you can see, by changing the composition of the customer base, increasing the proportion of sales coming from the "starfish" and "whale" customers, the retailer is able to increase overall gross profit margins from 19.4% to 20.56%, *all without a change in total sales volume.*

This concept of customer category management is vitally important to the further development of customer specific retailing. The actual numbers and spending breaks used in this type of reporting must be meaningful for each retailer and each industry.

The power of this scorecard lies in using it to record changes in the composition of the customer base over time. For example, a retailer could produce this report on a quarterly basis, as shown in Figure 5-7, measuring the changes in the customer categories quarter-to-quarter.

By looking at the report (Figure 5-7) we can see that "whale" customer households accounted for 2.2% of total households in the fourth quarter of Year 1. This proportion has increased to 3.7% of total customer households by the fourth quarter of Year 3. Now look at the corresponding change in sales represented by these "whales." In the fourth quarter of Year 1, the "whales" accounted for 13.6% of total sales; by the fourth quarter

Customer Category Management Scorecard — Quarterly Performance Report

Households*

		Year 1				Year 2				Year 3			
		1st Q	2nd Q	3rd Q	4th Q	1st Q	2nd Q	3rd Q	4th Q	1st Q	2nd Q	3rd Q	4th Q
<$24.99 SPW	Sharks	73.7%	74.4%	73.7%	73.1%	71.9%	69.5%	71.2%	69.9%	71.3%	71.6%	72.0%	71.0%
$25-$49.99 SPW	Cod	14.3%	14.4%	15.0%	14.5%	15.1%	15.9%	15.2%	14.3%	14.3%	14.3%	14.3%	14.4%
$50-$99.99 SPW	Starfish	10.3%	9.6%	9.7%	10.2%	10.7%	10.6%	10.0%	11.3%	11.0%	10.3%	10.2%	10.9%
$100+ SPW	Whales	1.7%	1.6%	1.6%	2.2%	2.3%	2.7%	2.4%	3.2%	3.4%	3.0%	2.9%	3.7%
	Total	100%	100%	100%	100%	100%	100%	100%	100%	100%	100%	100%	100%

Sales**

		Year 1				Year 2				Year 3			
		1st Q	2nd Q	3rd Q	4th Q	1st Q	2nd Q	3rd Q	4th Q	1st Q	2nd Q	3rd Q	4th Q
<$24.99 SPW	Sharks	27.4%	27.9%	27.5%	25.8%	25.2%	24.1%	25.0%	22.3%	22.8%	23.8%	24.5%	22.6%
$25-$49.99 SPW	Cod	26.1%	27.0%	27.5%	25.5%	25.8%	26.2%	26.4%	23.2%	22.8%	24.5%	24.5%	22.7%
$50-$99.99 SPW	Starfish	36.1%	34.8%	34.7%	35.0%	35.5%	34.0%	33.8%	36.1%	34.9%	33.8%	33.9%	33.7%
$100+ SPW	Whales	10.3%	10.3%	10.3%	13.6%	13.6%	15.8%	14.8%	18.3%	19.5%	17.8%	17.2%	21.0%
	Total	100%	100%	100%	100%	100%	100%	100%	100%	100%	100%	100%	100%

SPW = Spending Per Week
* Household data. Numbers shown represent the percent of total active households in quarter within each customer category.
** Sales data. Numbers shown represent the percent of total sales coming from households in each customer category.

These numbers would typically be reported both in actual numbers and in percentages, as shown, for internal company use. Author has used only percentages in this example, as actual numbers are meaningful only to the company from which they are derived. The percent changes evident in the households and in sales reflect the change in the composition of the customer base of this retailer. For example, in Quarter 1, Year 1, 1.7% of all households were "whales," by Quarter 1, Year 3, 3.4% of all households were now "whales."

* Data from "Sterling" Stores.

Figure 5-7

of Year 3 they accounted for 21% of total sales, a very substantial change. This change is represented graphically in Figure 5-8.

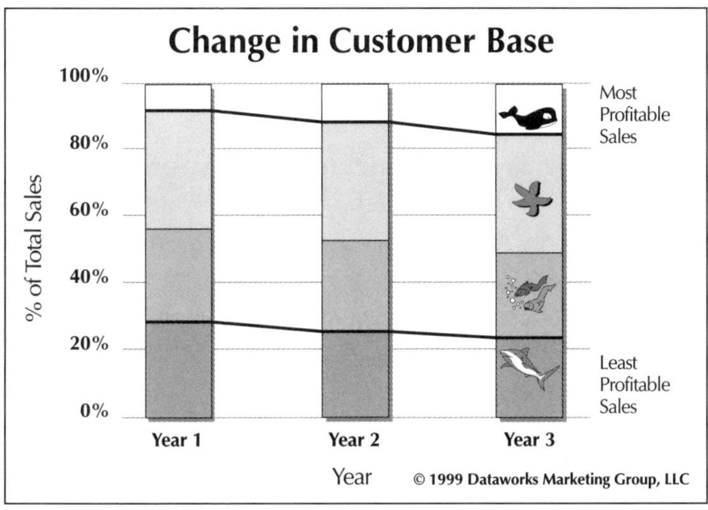

Figure 5-8

Some retailers have been able to triple the number of higher-spending customers in their customer base *with a corresponding gain to their gross profit margins.*

As we learned previously, higher-spending customers are more profitable than lower-spending customers. Thus, as a retailer can increase the number of these "whale" customers, profit gains will follow.

These types of changes can all happen under the surface of total sales. Profit gains emerge simply from changing the composition of the customer base; no top line sales gains are necessary.

Customer category management is perhaps the most important concept in this book. It is the key structural component arising from the foundation of customer information retailers are now capturing through their frequent shopper programs. As you continue through the book, we will be consistently referring back to this vital concept.

Even when retailers move to true customer specific retailing, they still must have a framework for reporting the data and information. Just as we do not report the movement of individual SKU's on our financial statements, we would not want to report individual customers' names either. Customer category management gives us a framework for summerizing meaningful data. This is a very powerful tool for those retailers who truly understand it *and are willing to begin managing their businesses by it.*

Building the New Enterprise Structure

Chapter 6: Organizational Structure

Ideally, a company's organizational structure should support its strategy.

In traditional retail companies, that strategy is product based. The strategy may be to offer the best selection of products or to be the lowest-priced in their channel. We need look no further than the organizational charts to see evidence of the prominence of products — frozen food departments, cosmetic departments, category managers, logistics managers, and so on. Entire organizations formed with products at their core.

In the new retail enterprise, the strategy is to develop one-to-one relationships with customers, tailoring the mix of products, prices, services, and information to each individual customer. The goal: to maximize the lifetime value of their customer base through improved retention of customers and extension of their purchasing.

As such, the new retail enterprise is organized around customers, not products. To bring this about requires that the entire organization re-engineer its processes to focus on the customer.

This is quite a challenge to any established retailer, particularly larger companies who have built their entire organizational structures and systems around products.

The new retail enterprise organization is still evolving. Many leading edge practitioners are wrestling with the best way to structure themselves in pursuit of their customer specific retailing goals. We are, however, seeing the broad outlines of what new capabilities need to exist within companies for them to be successful.

The customer specific retailer cannot exist without technology. Top managers of leading companies are comfortable with technology and how it can be used strategically. These companies are not enamored with the latest "gee-whiz" toys. They understand and use technology as a means to an end: improving the way they interact with their customers, and their ability to gather, understand, and use customer information.

The new retail enterprise is driven by people with a different "skill set" than the retailers of old. Many of the skills necessary for success in the new retail organization were simply not needed in the product driven retail company. Much of retail over the past several decades is characterized, for the most part, by a resounding lack of creativity. Time and again, retailers in all channels fall back on that tried and true method of item and price advertising. One needs only to read the financial pages to see that this has not been successful; and indeed, in today's hyper-competitive marketplace, reliance on this way of going to market is squeezing retailers' already slim margins to the breaking point.

The new battleground requires new skills: marketing skills must be honed for successful image and brand building. Analytical skills, combined with creativity, are needed to drill into the gigabytes of detailed customer information and to form new tactics. An understanding of technology is critical, as well as what today's information systems are capable of and how they can be used to build a new way of going to market. And lastly, strategy, a concept long forgotten by many mass retailers, is absolutely crucial for today's battles.

Marketing skills that the packaged goods companies have had for decades are now appearing at leading edge retailers. These companies recognize the fact that they now need true marketing skills. Many retailers have marketing departments, but in many cases, they have been little more than buying agents for mass advertising, used to support item and price advertising.

Retailers who have committed to this new way of going to market realize that they need people who can develop the concept of a brand around the store, as well as around the frequent shopper program. Indeed, these marketing people view their frequent shopper programs as brands. Stephen Zubrod, Vice President of Marketing for Baker's of Omaha, Nebraska, is a good example of this trend. Coming from a background in marketing on the manufacturing side, he is now using his skills to develop the concept of the retailer as a brand.

Zubrod has done a world class job of developing the Baker's Value card into a strong brand. He has built advertising and marketing campaigns around the card, all designed to promote and build recognition and value in the card program itself.

One of my favorite campaigns is the Baker's "Card Shark" promotion. Zubrod approached well-known personalities in the community and asked them to pose for photographs holding their Baker's Value card. The campaign was built around the theme of "card sharks." The ads appeared on television, billboards, and in many other places. The idea was to build the card as a brand in and of itself, and it was extremely successful.

Perhaps in the marketing department we will now have three separate positions: a person responsible for customer acquisition marketing strategies; another person responsible for customer extension (getting existing customers to spend more); and a person responsible for customer retention. The key point here is that for the first time a retailer can effectively measure true customer behavior in these areas, making these types of positions viable. If you can measure something (e.g., customer behavior), you can begin to manage it.

The marketing department can now begin creating different strategies and tactics for the various customer segments. The number of high-spending customers, cherry pickers, and defecting customers, can all be measured. The marketing budget is now allocated over these customer categories, where investment and performance can be measured to bring the highest return on investment for our marketing dollars.

Analytical skills are certainly important when dealing with a great deal of data. But this person in the organization must bring more than data analysis skills to the table. There are many retailers who generate report on top of report. Results gathered from the data must fulfill two important criteria: they must be *meaningful* and a*ctionable*. Far too many retailers produce data analysis that is interesting, even fascinating, but of no practical use.

As Peter Drucker reminds us, "A database, no matter how copious, is not information. It is information's ore. For raw material to become information, it must be organized for a task, directed toward specific performance, applied to a decision....The data users, whether executive or professional, have to decide what information to use, what to use it for, and how to use it. They have to make themselves information-literate."

This is probably one of the largest challenges awaiting the newcomer to customer specific retailing. The company's management must decide what new measures are important, what new metrics to begin using in how they run their business. Many retailers have customer information; those who understand it best are in the lead.

Creativity is called for when drilling down into the database. Almost all retailers who have some type of frequent shopper program have the same type of data: The winners will be those with the best understanding of that data, and the greatest willingness to use it. Time after time, experience has shown that those who think creatively when doing data analysis, and who possess some knowledge of retail operations in order to know what is useful, are the winners.

Lastly, some understanding of customer psychology is very important. Why do customers act the way they do? Certainly, basic psychology tells us that we should reward the behavior we seek. Thus, if we want higher-spending customers, we should reward higher spending.

For example, when Green Hills Farms ran its first associate reward program, some fascinating things were discovered. This reward program was fairly straightforward. Associate households could earn a 10% discount certificate, good on the order of their choice, for every $250 in accumulated purchases. At the conclusion of the program, we analyzed the results, i.e., the changes in behavior. It was then we noticed that this type of program creates a behavior-reward cycle. As the associate earned his or her discount, he or she would spend more when using it, thus achieving the next reward that much more quickly. This process accelerated through the program. In hindsight, this may seem to be very logical, but it was fascinating to see it develop. That type of learning was then transferred to other marketing programs for the general public, with very strong results.

While most companies do add some staff to support their frequent shopper efforts, the goal should be to minimize any added expense. Many times the goal is to re-direct what existing people are doing, to make use of the new information. For example, bookkeepers still produce weekly management reports, but use different information. Product category managers still purchase product, but now integrate customer category information to assist them in their decision making. Marketing people still design marketing programs, but are now able to truly measure their effectiveness.

Norman Mayne, of Dorothy Lane Markets, once told me, "I see which direction the big chains are going and then I run in the opposite direction!" His strategy is clear: to differentiate Dorothy Lane Markets from his larger competitors, by doing things differently — offering unique products, such as his Killer Brownies® or Coleman Natural Beef, and blowing away his competitors with customer service.

Moving in the direction of customer specific retailing offers companies of all sizes the opportunity to think creatively and strategically when they are formulating their plans. What type of basic incentive scheme will encourage customers to identify themselves each time they shop, and yet create a different marketing strategy from the competition? How can I begin tailoring my operations to different customer groups to increase their loyalty?

The customer specific retailer must acknowledge the new skills required of their organization and must either develop these capacities from within, or search outside the company.

Building the New Enterprise Structure

Chapter 7: Communication

In the new retail enterprise, communication with customers becomes a critical part of the business. As we create different rewards and offers for different customers, we must find new ways to communicate this information. No longer do the typical advertising media of newspaper, television, radio, and billboards accomplish all that we need.

The new retail enterprise requires communication vehicles that are truly customer specific, and yet are cost-effective and time efficient. In addition, these channels should allow for two-way communication: retailer to customer and customer to retailer. The goal is to build relationships with our customers, and successful relationships require communication between the parties.

Looking around the world, we see the development and use of a number of communication tools that support the above-noted criteria. We are discussing here only those communication vehicles that support true one-to-one relationships.

Direct Mail

Direct mail is the most well-known, and most used, communication tool employed by retailers today in support of their database marketing efforts. Direct mail is effective; people are familiar with it; and it can do a good job of communicating different messages to different customers. Most retailers with card programs that use direct mail, use it for some type of newsletter mailed to their customers or some type of targeted mailings, for example, specific offers to customers based on their purchasing history.

The experience of retailers around the world is that while direct mail is effective, it becomes very expensive when used on a regular basis. It also is not necessarily time-effective. It can sometimes take weeks for a mail piece to be planned, graphics developed, printed, addressed and mailed. Add to this the amount of time it may take to

No One Communication Vehicle is Right For All Customers.

Customers must be able to choose the communication channel that is right for them.

Figure 7-1

actually deliver it to the customer (days to weeks, depending on whether the retailer is using first class or bulk rate mail).

Interactive Voice Response Systems (IVR)

The next most widely used communication tool is some kind of interactive voice response (IVR) system. This is the same type of computer based telephony system that airlines, banks, credit card companies and many other businesses use. Customers simply call a telephone number, enter their frequent shopper card number, and the computer reads back their points balance or standing on whatever promotion is running at the time. This type of system will also support communicating other customer specific information, such as products and prices for individual customers.

POS Systems

The newest point of sale (POS) systems also serve as communication tools. For example, SASI's eXPERIENCE system can support individual customer specific messaging on the bottom of the receipt. This can be used to report back to customers their points balances or their spending totals toward earning their rewards. This can also be used to communicate other information to customers, such as their specials for the next week. Other POS systems from IBM, NCR, and ICL also may support limited customer specific information, for example points totals, being printed on receipts.

Kiosks

Kiosks of some sort have been on the scene now for several years, but with only minimal acceptance and use by customers. They do, however, play a critical role in the new retail enterprise. Kiosks are an important tool because they can communicate with customers as they are entering the store, not as they are leaving. Kiosks also are used to report customers' status on a points or reward program, but in addition, can communicate customer specific offers. The power of kiosks is magnified if they are tied to the POS system. Offers can be communicated through the kiosk and then delivered electronically (without paper) at the POS.

Albert Heijn, a leading supermarket retailer in the Netherlands, recently installed kiosks in each of their stores, to report back to customers their real time points balances on the frequent shopper program. Felpausch Food Centers, a chain located in Michigan, also has kiosks located in each of their stores. Customers can scan their cards at the kiosk and receive coupon offers based on their purchasing history.

Leevers used a simple, PC-based kiosk in support of their Helping Hands donation program. Leevers rebated 1% of a customer's spending during the program to a charity of the customer's choicc. Customers could scan their cards at the in-store kiosk to learn their spending total on the program.

Kiosks must be customer focused, not manufacturer driven. Early on, several kiosk systems appeared on the scene that were organized by companies who had gone to manufacturers for a pool of offers. By having access to the retailer's detailed customer information, these kiosks would target offers to customers, based on their purchasing history. Because these programs were funded by manufacturers, customers received competing brand offers, not necessarily appealing to their preferences.

To be successful, kiosks must also be quick to respond to a customer's card scan. It is suggested that a kiosk serve a very focused objective, for example, reporting back a customer's spending total or points balance. Kiosks that try to do everything (reporting totals, recipe selection, product directories, etc.) simply take too much time for the customer to use. Other customers will not wait.

Internet

Lastly is the Internet, perhaps the best and most comprehensive one-to-one communication vehicle. Web sites are already being tied to frequent shopper programs by a number of retailers.

Customers of Dick's Supermarkets in Madison, Wisconsin, can go to the company's web site and choose electronic coupons for products they may be interested in. By entering his or her frequent shopper number, the customer can receive these offers electronically the next time he or she shops. Customers of Dorothy Lane Markets can communicate via e-mail with the stores, relating their requests or experiences, in addition to ordering Dorothy Lane's Killer Brownies®! More and more retailers are beginning to link their frequent shopper programs with the Internet.

The new retail enterprise is using electronic based communication as their primary communication tool. Electronic based communications (IVR systems, POS, kiosks, Internet) are the most cost-effective and time-efficient.

Once the customer specific communication is assembled, typically derived from some type of marketing database software, it can be electronically moved to these communication vehicles at almost no cost. It is simply transferred over a network to the IVR, POS, kiosk or web site. In the new retail enterprise, the only place for paper based communication is in the store, output from a kiosk, or output from the POS system. Direct mail is used only sporadically to support specific marketing initiatives.

In addition to these electronic based communication vehicles being time-effective, they are also asynchronous. Customers can access these communications at whatever time is good for them. Unless customers happen to be in front of their televisions at the specific moment that a communication is aired, they will miss it. Not so with the Internet or an IVR system.

The new retail enterprises use each of these communication vehicles to support their goals. They realize that no one communication vehicle is right for all customers. Some people will read direct mail; others will throw it away. Some customers will use the Internet; others won't. Again, electronic based communication is extremely cost-effective to send out over different channels. Customers can then choose which communication channels are right for them.

It may be helpful to create a matrix of the different communication vehicles available to a retailer, and to what level of specificity they will go. This communication grid may look something like the example shown in Figure 7-2.

Communication Grid

	Internal to Store	External to Store
Mass	Signage PA Announcements	Newspaper Television Radio Billboards Share Mail
Customer Group Specific	Kiosk POS Monitor POS Receipt	Direct Mail IVR System Internet
Customer Specific	Kiosk POS Receipt POS Monitor	Direct Mail IVR Systems Internet

Figure 7-2

The beauty of using these new communication tools is that competitors lose sight of you. Essentially the new retail enterprise is practicing stealth marketing. Even if a competitor were to obtain a copy of a direct mail piece, they would have no way of knowing how many pieces went out, to whom, or how many different versions there were.

Building the New Enterprise Structure

Chapter 8: New Metrics and Economics

"Most important, if companies are really serious about delivering value and earning customer loyalty, they must measure it. And while senior executives may be daunted by the time and investment required to engineer an entire business system for high retention, they may have no alternative. Customer loyalty appears to be the only way to achieve sustainable superior profits."

Frederick F. Reichheld
The Quest for Loyalty

The new retail enterprise does not have to rely on product data as a standard by which to measure its business. We now have customer data, which is the essence of a customer focused company.

We are seeing a transition from old measurements, based on product movement or top line sales data, to new metrics which are now available to us through our customer information databases. For example, rather than measuring the number of transactions a retailer has per week, the new retail enterprise can measure the number of customer households shopping in their stores each week, a much more accurate view of what is truly happening.

Rather than looking at just department profitability yields, the customer specific retailer now looks at customer category profitability yields. Rather than practicing product category management, the new retailer practices customer category management. Instead of only viewing top line sales, the new enterprise measures same household purchasing. How many customers are maintaining their spending over time? How many are increasing? How many are decreasing?

One of the first new measurements that this new retail enterprise can make use of is more accurate accounting of its markdown or price reduction expense. Just about every retailer does some sort of price promotion. As such, there is a related price reduction expense. Almost every retailer has some type of process for accounting for this expense — but now it can be tied back to specific customers.

In the United States, it is becoming typical for retailers, especially supermarkets, to require their frequent shopper card for the customer to receive their advertised specials. Some retailers, usually those with the highest identification rates, require the card for the customer to receive any of their price reductions; in other words, all their markdown is moved to the card. As this happens, the retailer can now track this expense to the penny, and can associate the expense with individual customers.

Leading retailers have changed their accounting to reflect sales at full margin, expensing their markdown cost. By reflecting this on their financial statements, retailers now begin to focus on what their true markdown expense is, and thus begin to manage it. At the same time, this information now allows us to pull this expense information into our customer category management report. Are the rewards (markdown) that the different categories of customers are getting proportional to those customers' value to us?

Retailers not viewing their customer information in these ways are putting their future operations at risk. As we saw earlier in Chapter 5, retailers are now using the customer category management scorecard to measure changes within their customer base beneath the top line of their total sales.

Some time ago, Lisa Piron and I spent a day with a regional supermarket retailer who had asked us for assistance in moving their frequent shopper program to the next level. The retailer had been operating their card program for more than a year, and had run some different marketing programs designed to increase customer spending. This company was also faced with the situation of having several competitors who also had card programs and were doing a very good job with rewarding their best customers.

As we went through our client's data, it became very evident that there were problems, but not traditional ones. This company's top line sales were relatively stable, but there were massive changes occurring beneath the surface. Due to competitive pressures, this retailer had become more and more aggressive with item and price advertising, and as time went on, lost focus on their card program. Accordingly, they received the behavior they were rewarding. The number of higher-spending customers was dropping dramatically month-to-month, and these customers were being replaced with more and more cherry pickers. Top line sales stayed stable, but there were massive changes occurring under the surface. As this happened, the company's profit margins were weakening significantly. Same sales, but declining profits — all due to a change in the composition of the customer base.

As we saw in Chapter 5, Customer Category Management, our customers differ not only in their spending, but also in the profitability they offer to us as retailers. We know that if we can change the composition of our customer base, we can affect our profitability. The question now is, "How do we manage this change?" It is only when something can be measured that it can begin to be managed. The new retail enterprise actively manages their marketing rewards (markdown expense) to generate the best return on investment.

Using our information, we can now create a report such as the one shown in Figure 8-1. We can now see our sales, margins, marketing costs (markdown expense), and "projected" profit by customer category. It is through this type of information that the new retail enterprise can begin to align marketing expenditures with the different income streams offered by the different customer categories, to maximize profit yield.

In Figure 8-1, we are using an assumed gross profit margin of 30% (before markdown) to calculate the gross margin dollars of each customer category. This would be similar to using a company's overall gross margin Figure (before markdown) to calculate the gross margin dollars offered by a certain customer category. While this is not entirely accurate, due to the large differences in going-in gross margin by product (and whether it is on-deal or at regular cost), it does begin to point us in the direction of seeing the different levels of profitability offered by different customers.

Customer Category Profitability

Average SPW	Customer Category	Sales $	GM% (Full Margin)	GM $	Markdown $	Profit After Markdown	% Profit Before Exp.
	Unidentified	$ 10,000	30%	$ 3,000	$ 0	$ 3,000	30.0%
<$24.99	Tin	26,000	30%	7,800	3,500	4,300	16.5%
$25-$49.99	Bonze	24,000	30%	7,200	2,400	4,800	20.0%
$50-$99.99	Silver	30,000	30%	9,000	2,800	6,200	20.6%
$100 +	Gold	20,000	30%	6,000	1,300	4,700	23.5%
	TOTAL	***$110,000***	30%	$33,000	$10,000	$23,000	20.9%

SPW = Spending Per Week

For purposes of this report, we are using a going-in company gross margin of 30% for all customers. This is only an approximation of customers' profitability. The most accurate way to determine individual customer profitability is to track the cost and retail of each individual item purchased, but this is very difficult to do and very few retailers are attempting this. There is another reason for viewing the markdown dollars by customer group and individual customer, which will be explained in Chapter 14.

The information shown in this report does begin to indicate the differences in profitability that are offered by different customer groups. Typically, the lower-spending customers (for example, the Tin group) received a proportionally higher amount of markdown than do higher-spending customers (for example, Gold).

Figure 8-1

Certainly, the best way to report customer profitability is to track the cost and retail of each item and build up to customer profitability by tracking each item purchased, adding its profit. There is, however, an additional reason to track markdown expenditures by customer, other than reporting an "assumed" gross profit margin. This will be further addressed in Chapter 14.

One way to begin developing this is to view sales and markdown expenditures by customer category on a regular basis, perhaps as part of the regular financial reporting. This can take the shape of the information shown in Figure 8-2. This report states sales by customer category, expressed as a percentage of the total. Alongside, again reported by customer category, are the markdown expenses or marketing rewards received by each category, reported as a percentage of the total. Carrying this across, we can see the "differential" between a customer category's value to us in sales and what we provided them in markdown or marketing rewards.

One leading retailer uses a weekly management report similar to the sample shown in Figure 8-3. This report shows weekly sales activity by customer category and also divides the markdown expense across customer categories so that it can be monitored on a regular basis.

Perhaps one of the most important of the measures that have been developed to support the new retail enterprise is measuring same household purchasing behavior. Quarter to quarter, or year to year, how many of our customers are maintaining their spending? How many decreasing? How many increasing? How many are

Customer Category Management — Markdown Analysis Report

Current Financial Period

Average SPW	Customer Category	% of Total Sales	% of Total Markdown	Differential
	Unidentified	10%	0	n/a
<$24.99	Tin	24%	35%	11
$25-$49.99	Bonze	21%	24%	3
$50-$99.99	Silver	30%	28%	-2
$100 +	Gold	15%	13%	-2
	TOTAL	100%	100%	0

SPW = Spending Per Week

This report is simply a guide to understanding what each customer category is generating of total sales (expressed as a percentage of total) and what each customer category is receiving in total markdown expense (expressed as a percentage of total). This retailer has tied all markdown to their frequent shopper card, so unidentified sales (those done without a frequent shopper card) are at full margin (no markdown).

This report is an aid in determining how markdown is being spent — is it allocated across customer categories in approximation of the category's value in sales? For example, Tin customers are generating 24% of total sales and yet are receiving 35% of total markdown. Is this the most effective spend? Does it offer the best return on investment of the marketing (markdown) dollars?

Figure 8-2

defecting and from what customer category? This is perhaps one of the truest measures of performance available. A sample report is shown in Figure 8-4

This report is read in the following way: for example, of the 92 Gold customers in Quarter 2, 52 remained at the Gold level in Quarter 3, 35 dropped to the Silver level, 4 to the Bronze level, and so on. Likewise, of the 772 Bronze customers in Quarter 2, 2 moved up to the Gold level in Quarter 3, 89 moved to the Silver level, and 14 defected from the retailer.

Weekly Management Report

	Gold	Silver	Bronze	Tin	New	Unidentified	TOTAL
# of Households (from previous quarter)	384	1233	1597	7993			**11,256**
Sales	$48,707.00	$87,173.00	$56,700.00	$56,950.00	$1,485.00	$23,919.00	$274,934.00
% of Total Sales	17.7%	31.7%	20.6%	20.7%	0.5%	8.7%	
# of Transactions	1700	3233	2172	4129	67	2616	15,794
Average Order	$28.65	$26.96	$26.10	13.79	$22.16	$9.14	$17.41
$ Per Household	130.93	75.21	44.37	$22.98	30.31		
Household Information	372	1159	1278	2478	49		5336
% Shop (out of category)	97%	94%	80%	31%			
Frequency (visits per week)	4.57	2.79	1.7	0.6	1.75		
Markdown Expense	$3,765.00	$6,792.00	$4,585.00	$6,155.00	$371.00	—	$21,668.00
% of Total	17.4%	31.3%	21.2%	28.4%	1.7%		

Memo:				
Sales ID%	91.30%		Active HHs LY	5172
Trans. ID%	81.30%		Active HHs TY	5336
Def. Rate %	21.40%		Gain/Loss	164

Gold Customers = $100 + SPW (Spending Per Week)
Silver Customers = $50 - $99.99 SPW
Bronze Customers = $25 - $49.99 SPW
Tin Customers = < $24.99 SPW

*Data from "Haviland" stores presented on a per-store basis

Figure 8-3

Customer Category Management

Customer Migration Report

Quarter 2		Quarter 3				
		Gold	Silver	Bronze	Tin	Defected
Gold	92	52	35	4	1	0
Silver	556	24	476	28	26	2
Bronze	772	2	89	420	247	14
Tin	3980	2	36	350	2943	649
	5400	80	636	802	3217	665

This report is read this way: of the 556 Silver customers in Quarter 2, 476 of them remained Silver customers in Quarter 3, 24 of them moved up to Gold, 28 dropped to Bronze and 26 declined to the Tin level. Of the 556 Quarter 2 Silver households, two of them defected from the retailer.

We can now see in total that of the 5400 households in Quarter 2, 665 customers have defected, giving this retailer a quarter-to-quarter defection rate of 12.3% (5400/665).

Figure 8-4

Measuring and managing customer retention can have a dramatic impact on a retailer's business. Retaining a customer is every bit as valuable, and inevitably more profitable, than luring in new customers. World class practitioners are measuring their customer defection rates on a regular basis. What is important here is not necessarily each number, which represents a snapshot of the business at a specific point in time, but what the trend in those numbers is over time. If a retailer's customer defection rate is steadily climbing, there are problems.

Likewise, a declining defection rate is a good sign that the retailer is building their sales base.

The new retail enterprise measures and manages the life cycle of its customers.

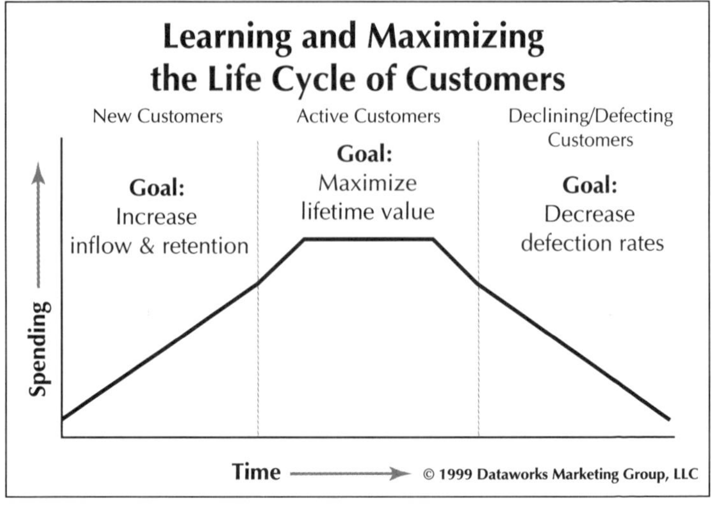

Figure 8-5

Every retailer has new customers coming through their doors each week. The goal now is to improve retention of those customers and increase their spending. It has been found in the United States that the typical supermarket loses approximately 50% of new customers after the first shopping visit. By the third visit, nearly 70% of that group of new customers is gone. Now that a retailer can identify these customers, it is possible to design and implement programs and processes to improve the retention and spending of this customer segment.

Every retailer has existing, active customers shopping with them. The goal in this area is to improve these customers' spending and to improve retention of them over time. Customer category management provides the measurement tool for use in benchmarking the changes in this customer group.

Every retailer has customers who are in the process of declining in their purchasing, or defecting from the retailer. The goal here is to lower the defection rate, thus building the sales base over time.

> *"Customer defections have a surprisingly powerful impact on the bottom line. They can have more to do with a service company's profits than scale, market share, unit costs, and many other factors usually associated with competitive advantage. As a customer's relationship with the company lengthens, profit rises. And not just a little. Companies can boost profits by almost 100% by retaining just 5% more of their customers."*
>
> Frederick F. Reichheld and W. Earl Sasser, Jr.
> *Customer Loyalty*

In addition to being able to see the life cycle of our customers, we need to develop metrics to measure and quantify their lifetime value to us. Retailers who operate at this level, capture 90% of sales through their card, and are able to maintain this level of information capture over time, have the information necessary to evolve to these new business metrics.

Eventually, retailers will be segmenting their customers based on profitability rather than simply their purchasing. There are basically two ways to arrive at customer profitability: building from item level profitability up, or extrapolating customer profitability from the customer's purchases and markdown.

While it is possible to get to this level, and indeed several retailers are almost there, it remains to be seen how effectively this information can be used. While customers are aware of what they spend, they are not aware of their profitability to the retailer. It is possible to change customers' behavior with regard to spending; it is less clear if we can change a customer's profitability as overtly.

As we have seen, one price for all is no longer the most efficient, profitable way for a retailer to go to market. In the customer specific retail enterprise, pricing and marketing are designed to skew spending, effecting a change in the composition of the customer base and increasing the number of higher-spending customers. Marketing expenditures are now viewed as investments in maximizing the lifetime value of our customer base.

There are four fundamental ways to increase the lifetime value of our customer base: 1) increase customer spending; 2) increase the retention rate of our customers; 3) increase the length of time they shop with us (lifetime); or; 4) simply increase the number of customers we have. Some might say that these are the same objectives a traditional retailer has. This is a correct comment, with one important exception: *the traditional retailer has no way of measuring the return on investment from their expendi-*

tures other than by top line sales or total profitability. The customer specific retailer can measure expenditures and changes in performance down to the individual customer. This is inherently a much more efficient way to go to market. This type of system will produce a much greater return on investment than mass marketing programs.

Using customer category management, we can now segment our customer base and market to each segment individually. For example, we can design programs to increase the spending and retention of new customers. The customer specific retailer is indeed operating this way. These companies are measuring their customer base, using the types of tools that are described here, and have organized themselves, their operations and their marketing, around this data. They are actively managing the life cycle of their customers.

It is necessary to look beyond the top line of sales when doing a return on investment analysis of these new types of marketing programs. We must look at the lifetime value of the targeted customer segments. Have we improved customer retention rates, increased their spending, drawn more customers into this segment?

Measuring the life cycle and lifetime values of our customers can have substantial implications for our accounting practices. Our systems must change to reflect this new information. Just as companies have reflected the value of their product inventory on their balance sheets, the new customer specific retail enterprise can reflect the value of their customer base.

In addition, in the past our accounting systems and our operational reporting systems have functioned independently in many companies. As we integrate our customer information into our financial reports and into our operations (buying, etc.), we are bringing the two together. We are seeing leading retailers beginning to implement data warehousing solutions, or expanding their present efforts, to create one source of data for all purposes. In this environment, financial data, as well as merchandising and operational data, are all pulled from the same source, meaning that we will now be able to fully integrate our customer information across all reporting.

Section 4: Working and Shopping in the New Retail Enterprise

Using the new metrics developed in Section Three, the customer specific retail enterprise has total control over its numbers. There are no surprises; the new retail

How do we use all this information?

enterprise knows from which customers the sales came, or did not materialize. By measuring retention rates of customers, the new enterprise can more effectively evaluate its ongoing marketing and operational efforts.

Supporting these new metrics are the new communication vehicles. Using these new channels, the retailer no longer has to think in terms of communicating with a nameless horde of consumers through mass advertising. The customer specific retailer can now communicate individually with their customers.

For me, this next section is the fun and creative part of the new retail enterprise. It is only by having these new measures, and using these new communication technologies, that we can shift the playing field. No longer is it necessary to have multi-million dollar advertising budgets — not when we can send a personalized letter to our top customers and include a special offer that we know is meaningful to them...and then measure the response.

The new retail enterprise is shifting their marketing strategies to support their customer category management efforts. What new marketing programs can be devised to increase the number of higher-spending customers? What can we do to increase our customer retention rate? What is not possible to do for thousands of customers becomes suddenly doable when focusing on only a handful at store level.

In addition to the surge in creativity now possible in retailing, there are serious implications here for other segments of the retail industry.

As retailers gather and understand their customer data, and integrate it with their merchandising strategies, they are creating a new world for the consumer packaged goods companies. No longer are the manufacturers necessarily in control. Information is power, and the customer specific retailer has a great deal of information and understanding.

Rather than create yet another front in the tensions already existing in retailer-manufacturer relations, there is a unique opportunity for the two to work together for their true mutual benefit.

It is now necessary for retailers and manufacturers to think strategically. What types of incentives will produce the desired results, and yet differentiate the retailer from competitors? What advantages do a retailer's technologies and information systems offer compared to competing firms? How can they be used to create a sustainable advantage?

The customer specific retail enterprise is still developing, still evolving. May you have fun along the way!

Working and Shopping in the New Retail Enterprise

Chapter 9: Marketing and Advertising

Some time ago, I spent a day with an executive team from one of the leading share mail companies. We had a fascinating discussion on how the retail move into frequent shopper programs was going to affect their business and how they could develop new strategies and competencies to cope. As the day went on, it became clear that as retailers begin more serious adoption of customer specific marketing tactics, their advertising strategies will change.

Although strategies are changing, the total amount of marketing expenditures by these leading practitioners is not. Indeed, in some cases, retailers are finding they can substantially reduce the monies spent on traditional advertising without any adverse effect on their business. Our discussion that day led us to develop the graphic shown in Figure 9-1 to represent the changes that retail marketing budgets and strategies are undergoing.

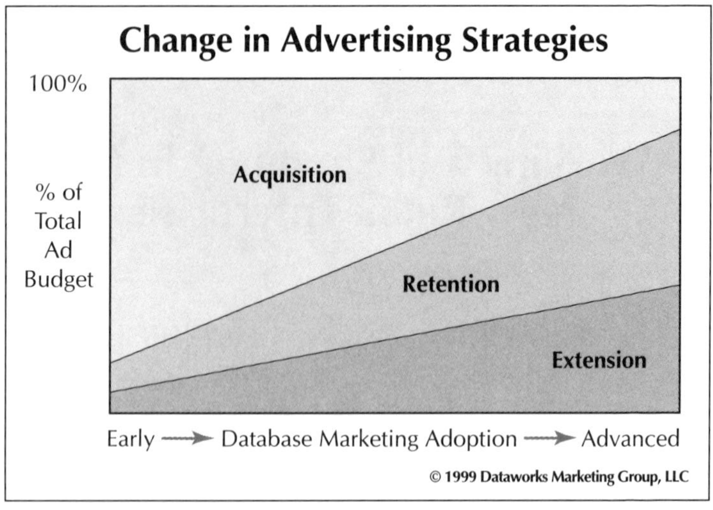

Figure 9-1

Retailers have historically focused their advertising efforts on customer acquisition. Indeed, the true purpose of the weekly advertisement, filled with products and prices, is to bring customers to the store. Many retailers justify the sums they spend on weekly item and price marketing by viewing it as a reward for their existing customers. To a degree they are correct, but these same customers are also subsidizing a great deal of economic waste in a retailer's advertising plan. Very little thought, or investment, is made in the area of retaining existing customers or getting them to spend more. This really is no surprise, because until recently, retailers had no way to truly measure their customer behavior.

John Wanamaker, known as the man who created the first department store, is renowned in the field of marketing for his statement, "I know that half my advertising is wasted...I just don't know which half!" Wanamaker spoke a truth that marketers have had to accept and live with — until now.

One of the key benefits of gathering and using customer data is that it provides a much better, more accurate measurement tool for retailers to use in evaluating their traditional practices. Retailers can now approach their newspaper circular advertising armed with this new information.

Typical retailers distribute some type of advertising circular in the newspapers or by share mail. It is now a relatively easy process to compare customer category information to distribution area. For example, if a newspaper is distributed by zip code (as many are) the retailer can now measure, by zip code, how many "gold" or "tin" customers they have in each area. Distributing several thousand ads into an area where the retailer is getting few "gold" customers may not be a good return on investment. It may be much more cost effective to terminate the ad distribution in that area and simply direct mail the ads to those customers.

The next phase in this cost reduction strategy is to look at the number of pages in the ad and the colors. Retailers putting out 12-page ads find that they can reduce them to eight pages with no loss of business. Likewise, retailers using full color throughout the ad find that they can reduce them to two or three colors inside, at a great savings. Our experience has been that it is the rare retailer who cannot realize substantial savings in their traditional newspaper advertising.

Some retailers will balk at the idea of reducing their ad pages and/or circulation. These retailers believe that their print ad is a profit center, and indeed, depending on how they do their accounting, it may well be. Many retailers sell their ad space: manufacturers pay for placement in the ad, with the fee dependent on placement and size of their feature. These retailers then book these fees as revenue, in some cases turning a profit after paying for their print and distribution costs.

Manufacturers' willingness to pay for ad placement is on a downward trend. Many have moved to Procter and Gamble's accrual method; retailers earn a specified amount of money for each case of P&G product they sell in a year. These monies are then available to the retailer the following year to promote P&G products. No ad fees or other promotional monies are available; everything is in the fund, which is tied to case movement.

As the industry moves even more toward pay for performance in their promotional monies, perhaps retailers' resistance to altering their print advertisements will diminish, especially in light of the customer information now available.

We can now begin to measure the shrink in our print advertising. Retailers can now begin to produce the type of report shown in Figure 9-2.

Customer Category Management Report — Advertising Matrix

Average SPW	Customer Category	Sales $	Profit After Markdown	# of Households	Ad Inserts Cost (.08 ea)	Profit After MD & Adv.	% Profit After MD & Adv.
<$24.99	Tin	$ 26,000	$ 4,300	7,100	$ 560.00	$ 3,740	14.4%
$25-$49.99	Bronze	24,000	4,800	1,510	120.80	4,679	19.5%
$50-$99.99	Silver	30,000	6,200	1,070	85.60	6,114	20.4%
$100 +	Gold	20,000	4,700	320	25.60	4,674	23.4%
	TOTAL	***$100,000***	$20,000	10,000	$800.00	$19,200	19.2%
	Waste:			40,000	$3,200.00		
	Total Ad Inserts:			50,000			

The retailer is distributing 50,000 inserts each week at a total cost of $4,000 per week (.08 cost each).

With 10,000 active households the retailer now knows that it is wasting 40,000 inserts each week for a total waste of $3,200 per week, or $166,400 per year!

The retailer also realizes that the lower-spending customers (for example, Tin) are even less profitable when they apply the cost of advertising to these households. Advertising to the Tin customer category costs 2% of sales; advertising to the Gold customers costs only 0.1%.

Figure 9-2

This report has a two-fold purpose. Not only does it determine the "shrink" in our print advertising (newspaper inserts), but it also shows the cost of our print advertising by customer category. This cost can then be subtracted from the profit of each category so that we can reflect profitability after marketing expenses (marketing rewards, markdown expense, and advertising expense) by customer category.

What to do with this information? It is typically this type of report that leads retailers to do some type of distribution analysis, explained earlier. At the very least, knowing the "shrink" that exists causes retailers to constantly monitor their advertising expenditures to ensure that they are getting a favorable return on investment.

With regard to all mass advertising efforts (newspaper, radio, or television), while the medium may remain the same, the message changes. Leading practitioners have started changing the message from item and price advertising to promoting the benefits of their card program. Rather than a front page having eight item and price features on it, retailers reduce the number of specials to four, for example, and devote space to promoting their current card-based marketing program.

The same holds true for radio, television, and billboard advertising. The medium remains, but the message changes, to begin building the card program as a brand, relating all the benefits of membership. For example, rather than a radio spot or television commercial being devoted to items and prices, some portion of it now is given to building recognition and awareness of a retailer's frequent shopper card program. The advertising features constant reminders to customers of the benefits of getting and using the retailer's card; they promote partners programs, reward programs, and so on. In short, they build value in the card program itself.

The advertising and promoting of the different marketing programs retailers run through their card is very important. As retailers promote their reward programs, for example, a free Thanksgiving turkey program, customers are essentially self-selecting whether or not they choose to participate. By not publicly promoting these types of programs, retailers are missing a golden opportunity to attract new customers who can become high-spending, loyal customers.

This becomes very important in markets where multiple, competing retailers have frequent shopper programs. How can you differentiate your program from the competitors'? Some of this has to do with the basic incentive scheme strategy, but the values put into the card, and then how this is communicated to the customer, become the defining factors.

Let me provide an example from Syracuse, New York, where Green Hills Farms is located. Green Hills competes in a market where three competitors also have frequent shopper card programs: Wegmans, Price Chopper, and Peter's, an independent chain. All of these retailers tie their markdowns to card use; the customer must use his or her card to receive the advertised specials.

Faced with this challenge, Green Hills ran a series of ads designed to highlight the differences in the card programs, to show customers that all frequent shopper card programs are not equal. A sample ad from that series is shown in Figure 9-3.

As retailers evolve through the continuum toward customer specific retailing they begin to view their marketing strategies differently. They now see that they have different types of customers, and that their marketing tactics can be differentiated by customer segment.

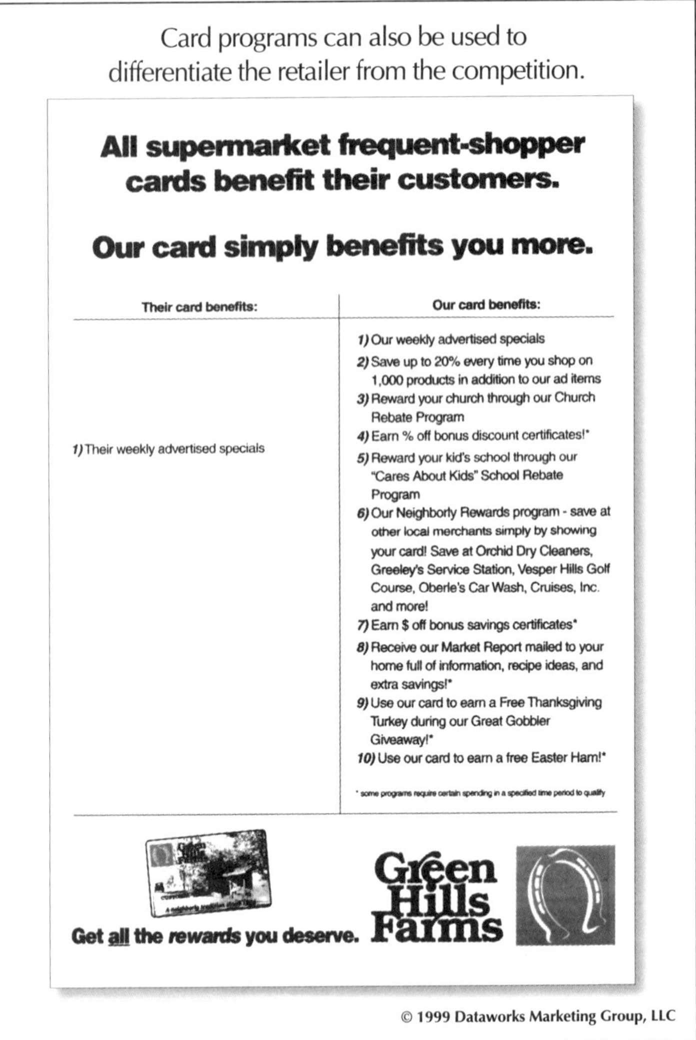

Figure 9-3

They learn that they can spend less on customer acquisition — that it is more effective and more profitable to concentrate on increasing the retention and spending of the customers they already have. The retailer is taking the savings possible in traditional advertising, and redirecting it into customer retention and extension efforts.

We need to teach our customers how to do business with us. The customer specific retailer is changing the way customers have normally shopped and is also changing the reward structure. In the past, customers were gratified with short-term rewards — our price reductions. We are now changing this to long-term rewards — rewarding our customers for their shopping with us over time. This is a different way to operate, not only for us as retailers, but also for our customers.

One of the questions I am frequently asked is, "When I develop a card program, can I drop advertising?" My answer is an unequivocal maybe.

I have come to believe that the issue of typical item and price newspaper advertising must be viewed in terms of the retail operation itself, and also of the competitive environment.

Retailers who are truly unique, such as Dorothy Lane Markets, have been able to successfully drop item and price advertising with no ill effect. Other, more traditional supermarkets have ceased advertising, only to see their sales volume immediately begin to drop, and have rushed back to it.

Retailers such as Felpausch Food Centers now make their weekly ad available only in their stores, realizing significant cost savings from not having to distribute their print ads.

Another example comes from an experience at Green Hills. For more than a year, we had successfully dropped our newspaper advertising. As time went on, we found it increasingly hard to maintain our volume. We noticed that, while we were still attracting new customers to the store, we were not getting as many as we had previously. During this time, the environment in the market also became much more competitive. Customers in the Syracuse market would receive their Sunday papers, and they would contain no fewer than seven, to as many as 10, major supermarket ads. None of these ads had fewer than eight pages; some ran to 24 pages; and all featured a lot of color. Green Hills was almost forced to return to advertising simply to be seen as still being in the game. By not appearing in the Sunday paper, we began to lose presence in customers' minds.

There is no right or wrong with regard to traditional advertising. The difference now is that retailers have much more information available to them with which to make more informed decisions. It is those retailers who are willing to experiment who will realize some level of savings, which can then be redirected into their customer specific retailing efforts.

What happens regarding in-store marketing is every bit as important in the success of a retailer's program as the external advertising and marketing.

I once visited a well-known supermarket chain in the Mid-west. The chain had had a card program in place for almost two years, and during my visit we toured one of their newest stores. The operators were very proud of this store, and it was beautiful. It featured large perishable departments, prepared foods and everything a modern supermarket should have. I walked through the entrance and up and down several aisles before I found a sign that told me that this store had some type of frequent shopper card. However, the sign didn't tell me where to go to get one or what the benefits were; I was left to figure that out for myself.

The point here is quite simple: if you have a frequent shopper program, and you are serious about it, you need to inform your customers! As retailers, we are all guilty of assuming that our customers know all about what we have to offer them. Sadly, this is not the case.

Too often, retailers take for granted that customers "just know" all we have to offer. Time and again, customers walking into stores that have a card program see no mention of it upon entry. How are our rushed, harried customers expected to know: 1) that the store has a frequent shopper card, 2) what the benefits of having and using the card are, and 3) how and where to get a card?

Certainly, during the launch of their programs, many retailers have well-decorated sign-up tables at the front of the store, capturing customers' attention immediately. Come back a few weeks later, however, and the announcements have long disappeared; the customers must fend for themselves.

Esselunga, a medium-sized supermarket chain in Milano, Italy, does a superb job of promoting their card program. At the entrance to their stores there is a sign-up booth —

a permanent, staffed fixture. The booth has clear and effective signs; a customer cannot help but notice that Esselunga has a loyalty card, what the benefits are, and that they can sign up for it immediately. Not only can new customers sign up for a card at the booth, but existing card holders can check on their point status and also redeem points for their rewards.

Signage related to a card program must continue beyond the front entrance. The message that the store has a card program, what the benefits are, and where to sign up for a card, must be displayed throughout the store.

In addition, if the card is required for price discounts, or to earn points, this message must also be clearly and prominently displayed. Bi-Lo, when they launched their card program, did an excellent job with their shelf signs. The product description, the price with the card, and the savings were very clearly displayed. They continued their message throughout the store, from floor decals of their Bonus card, to ceiling danglers, to signage at the check-out area. There was no doubt as to the features of their card program.

Signage throughout the store is critical. Do you have signs announcing your card program to new customers as they enter your store? Do you have signs around the store devoted to the benefits of your card? Do you tell customers where to go in the store to sign up for a card? If you have moved your markdown to the card, do your price signs clearly show this? If it is a points program, is this clear to your customers?

Working and Shopping in the New Retail Enterprise

Chapter 10: Customer Category Management in Practice

Using the tools discussed in the previous section, we now have an entirely new way to view and operate our businesses.

Retailers who have enough quality detailed customer information can begin measuring and managing the life cycle of their customers. As we saw in Section Three, we can divide the life cycle of our customers into three categories: new customers, existing/active customers, and declining/defecting customers. By overlaying this schematic with the customer category management scorecard, we now have a new way to look at and run our retail businesses, as illustrated in Figure 10-1.

As we begin doing this, we should keep in mind both our short-term and long-term goals. In the short term, the customer specific retailer is using a mix of rewards, incentives, services, and so on to increase the lifetime value of the customer base. In addition, the retailer is taking a longer-term view, continuously learning what

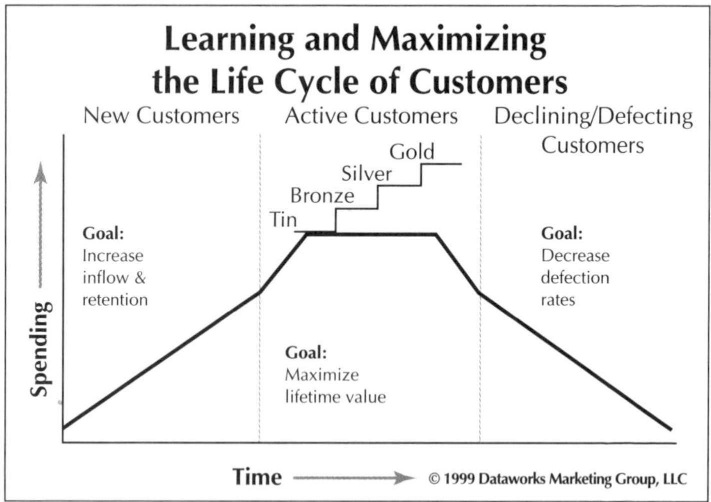

Figure 10-1

appeals to their individual customers, in order to continuously improve the personalized shopping experience that customer specific retailing has as its goal.

We now see that we have not simply one customer base, but in effect, six customer segments we can market to. And, because each of these segments is different, we can devise different marketing strategies and tactics designed to maximize each segment.

New Customers

When studying supermarkets across North America, we see that, on average, the typical supermarket experiences very poor retention of new customers who come through their doors for the first time. On average, 40-50% of new customers never return to the retailer again. By the third visit, only 25-30% of the original group is still shopping at the supermarket.

What can be done to slow this loss? One leading retailer has designed a new customer program to address this area.

A customer entering this retailer's store for the first time is greeted by signs inside the entrance informing the customer that this store has a frequent shopper program, and that the customer need only stop by the customer service desk to sign up. On inquiring at the service desk, the customer is given a very brief application to complete. While this is being done, one of the managers (they rotate days) is called to the desk to meet the customer. The manager reviews a short brochure of the store, which explains the store hours, forms of payment accepted, services offered, etc.

Also in this brochure is a discount certificate good for the customer to use that day. This discount certificate is a graduated savings incentive. If the customer spends $25 that day, he or she can save $3; if he or she spends $50, the savings is $7.50, and so on. The idea is to immediately bring the customer on board with the idea that this retailer rewards shopping and loyalty.

In addition, a second offer is presented to the customer by the manager. The customer is informed that by spending $300 in the next six weeks, he or she can earn $30 in free groceries. The two offers are meant to provide both a short-term and a long-term reward. If the customer has time, the manager offers to give him or her a brief tour of the store.

That's not all. The retailer also enters this new customer in a direct mail program. Each week, for the next four weeks, the customer will receive a letter from the retailer explaining a unique aspect of their stores, for example, explaining the scratch bakery or some other area. Included in the mailing each week is an offer, for example a certificate for a dozen free donuts from the scratch bakery.

The final mailing includes a brief survey, which the customer is asked to complete and drop at the store the next time he or she is shopping. The survey addresses store operations, product quality, etc. It is surprising how many of these surveys are completed and returned to the store.

This entire effort is directed toward retaining and increasing the spending of new customers. This retailer understands that it is difficult to break a customer's old shopping habits, and that it is hard for a customer to begin shopping in a new store that he or she is unfamiliar with.

Yes, this program represents an investment in these customers. But remember, the rewards are not offered to everyone. These things are done for a handful of people, new customers only. And, since the rewards are tied to spending, the customers essentially self-select whether or not they wish to participate.

Some pessimists will be thinking, "How many customers will actually take the time to go through this whole process?" You would be surprised. More than 90% of new customers are willing to take the time to speak with the manager; many of them actually comment that they have never experienced anything like this before, and that they think it is wonderful for the retailer to be so interested in their customers.

What is the return on this investment? This retailer is now retaining fully 10% more new customers after one year than it was previously. If the retailer has an inflow of 50 new customers each week per store, that's five additional customers gained each week, 260 customers gained after one year. If you calculate that the average customer spends even $20 per week, that's an increase in sales of $5,200 per week, per store ($270,400 per year!) simply from this new customer program initiative.

Creative retailers can also look outside their industry for other ideas. During a trip to Brazil some months ago, I stayed at an Inter-Continental Hotel. While there, I signed up for their Six Continents Club. As a member, I receive special services, club floors, etc., when staying at any of their hotels. Several months later, I stayed at Inter-Continental Hotels in London, Sydney, and Tokyo during a trip around the world. In each of the hotels I was given a very warm greeting and directed to the club floor for a special check-in.

In Sydney, on entering my room I found a letter from the hotel manager, welcoming me to the hotel and offering me a choice of a free room service breakfast or a pay movie. In addition, I was supplied with a set of personalized stationery, with my name laser printed on specially prepared hotel stationery.

When I arrived in Tokyo, I was again greeted warmly and directed to the club floor for check-in. Waiting for me in my room was a chilled bottle of wine and a small cheese and fruit plate.

These things were all part of Inter-Continental's new customer program. Rewards and recognition are incentives for me to stay with Inter-Continental during my future travels. What was impressive was that this worldwide hotel chain must have excellent database capabilities to have been able to track me as I moved from hotel to hotel around the world within a matter of days. The technology bar is being raised very quickly in all industries!

Existing / Active Customers

Every retailer has existing customers shopping with them — customers who have been shopping and will continue to shop with the retailer. The goal for this segment of our customer base is to increase the spending of these customers, as well as the length of time they are shopping at a higher level, thus maximizing their lifetime value.

The concept here is quite simple. As we have reviewed earlier, higher-spending customers are more profitable than lower-spending customers. This is all about increasing the number of higher-spending customers in our customer base. It is that simple and it is that powerful. Many retailers overlook this, wishing to make it more complicated than it really is.

Before we start dreaming of ways to begin accomplishing this goal, we need a measurement system by which to gauge our efforts. Let's go back to our customer category management (CCM) scorecard and overlay this onto the customer life cycle chart. We will use the CCM scorecard to track how successful we are in accomplishing our goal.

In addition to providing additional incentive for customers to use their frequent shopper cards, marketing programs, as explained in Chapter 2, also serve as an incentive for increasing customers' purchasing. Almost all marketing programs discussed in this book do a very good job of providing strong incentives for customers to centralize their shopping with a particular retailer in return for earning some type of reward.

We have to realize that within each customer category there are some customers who are devoting almost all their shopping to the retailer, while others are spending a great deal more in total, and are giving the retailer only a portion of their total purchases. For example, in the Silver category ($50-$100 a week average spending) there may be an elderly couple who spends $60 per week on supermarket products, giving all their purchases to one retailer. Another household — a family — spends more than $200 per week in total, but is only giving this retailer $75 a week on average. Both are Silver level customers but each has different potential. How does the retailer provide incentive for both?

Colleen Butler-Rodriguez of Ukrop's in Richmond, Virginia, has voiced a related concern. It is all well and good to provide strong incentives to high-spending customers, but what about people on a fixed income, for example senior citizens? Isn't the retailer who focuses solely on $100-a-week customers discriminating, or at least risking offending an important demographic group?

There are ways to address this, commonly done through different levels or tiers added to the marketing programs. Let me provide an example of a marketing program that addresses each of the above concerns.

The first year of the Green Hills Farms free Thanksgiving turkey program, the reward was very simple: any customer who spent more than $500 in the 10 weeks leading up to Thanksgiving received a free turkey. The first year's program was very successful, but we received two general comments when it was over. The first came from some seniors who stated that they had shopped with the store for years, but because they were older and on a limited income, they simply did not spend $50 a week. They thought the program was a wonderful way to reward and recognize customers, but they asked if we could do something different for them.

The second comment came from several customers who spent $1,000 during the program. They asked if they could receive two free turkeys because they spent twice the amount required. Smart people!

Several years and several turkey programs later, the Green Hills free Thanksgiving turkey program consists of four different spending levels. The first, marketed for seniors, requires that the customer spend $300 in the 10 weeks. In return, the seniors can earn a free, fresh turkey breast. Seniors are asked to sign up for this program at the customer service desk. They are then tagged in the database so that they can be tracked separately. The idea is not to offer this program to everyone!

The basic reward program remains the same: customers can earn a free, fresh turkey in return for spending $500 during the course of the program. Customers who spend $750, however, can earn both a turkey and a fresh, decorated Christmas wreath.

Customers who spend $1,000 or more during the program receive not only a free, fresh turkey but also a beautiful 7′ to 9′ tall Christmas tree, valued at $45. This program has proven so popular that some customers have driven back to the store to tell us that their trees are the most beautiful Christmas trees they've ever had.

This marketing program has evolved into four levels, each addressing a certain customer category segment. Each level rewards customers for maintaining their spending, but also provides a strong incentive to move up — to increase their spending in order to earn the next higher level reward.

The return on investment of any of these marketing programs must be measured differently than past types of promotional efforts. This is why the new metrics, our

CCM scorecard, and measurements such as customer retention, become so important. These new marketing programs are not necessarily intended to drive top line sales; they are intended to increase the number of higher-spending customers within the customer base, and increase customer retention rates and lifetime values.

Remember, gross profit margins follow higher customer spending. When a retailer can increase the number of higher-spending customers as a proportion of the total customer base, profit margin improvements will follow.

So how does a retailer analyze these marketing reward programs? Certainly, being retailers, we still look at the top line of sales. But, being customer specific retailers, we must now look at changes in our CCM scorecard, our profit margins, and our customer defection rates. These factors now become the guiding indicators.

We must also realize that, try as we might, we cannot be all things to all people. As retailers begin recognizing and rewarding their better, higher-spending customers, a sorting process takes place in the customer base. Reward programs do not appeal to everyone; some customers respond by spending more to earn the rewards; others decrease their spending, preferring to cherry pick the other retailers in the market. This sorting process is a natural outcome of rewarding and recognizing customers' shopping behavior. Done properly, it effects a substantial change in the customer base, increasing the proportion of higher-spending, more profitable customers.

Card based marketing programs: defined-length promotions designed to alter customers' shopping behavior by establishing spending goals and rewards.

Marketing programs, as defined above, accomplish two very important tasks. First, they begin to alter customer shopping behavior, increasing the number of higher-spending customers. Second, they provide yet another incentive for customers to obtain and use the retailer's frequent shopper card, giving the retailer more information.

Marketing promotions are limited only by a retailer's creativity. It is important to have some goal for your program, and to measure the results of it upon completion. Too many retailers run different marketing programs simply because it's the "thing to do," because they're copying other retailers around the country, or because they have some vague notion about increasing customer loyalty.

Rather than devoting an entire book to specific marketing programs, let me present some of the more noteworthy programs that have become popular around the world, and explain what benefits they bring to the retailer.

"Reward Yourself" Program

To the best of my knowledge, this program originated at Lees Supermarket in Westport, Massachusetts. Customers can earn discount certificates based on their purchasing in a specified period of time.

For example, during a six-week program, customers spending between $200 and $399 earn a 5% discount certificate to use on a future order of their choice. Customers spending between $400 and $599 earn a 10% discount certificate and customers spending more than $600 earn a 20% discount certificate.

These types of programs typically generate an increase in the number of households spending at those thresholds, compared to the same time period a year earlier. They also may produce a significant sales gain during the redemption period, when customers are using their reward certificates.

"Write Your Own Ad" Program

Otherwise known as the 5% program, this program was created and first run by Green Hills Farms in the fall of 1995, and has since been run by any number of companies around the country.

As it was initially run, this program rewards customers with a 5% discount certificate for each $250 they accumulate in purchases during the three-month program. The reward certificates are mailed to the customers each week as they are earned.

This program substantially increased spending among those customers who had shopped during the same three-month period the year before. An additional lesson was that the highest-spending customers valued this type of reward structure much more than they valued weekly advertised specials. These customers very much liked being able to purchase the brands and sizes they wanted, and still be able to save through this reward program.

The majority of retailers who have run this program may not have realized how to properly analyze the results. This program's primary goal is not to drive top line sales, but to increase the number of higher-spending customers beneath the surface.

Free Thanksgiving Turkey

This program has proven to be quite popular in the United States over the past several years. It is a very straightforward program: by spending a specified amount with the retailer in a certain number of weeks leading up to Thanksgiving, customers can earn a free turkey.

While many retailers run a free turkey program, few do it correctly. By this, I mean that some retailers offer turkeys either free (to qualifying customers) or at full, regular price. Some retailers try to have it both ways. They run a free turkey program, and then price promote turkeys during the last week or two leading up to the Thanksgiving holiday. These retailers are shooting themselves in the foot. By price promoting turkeys, they are devaluing their offer to their best customers.

Other retailers, afraid of how many turkeys they may end up giving away, decide on a stealth/surprise course of action. In the second or third week before the holiday, they mail their best customers a certificate for a free turkey. By not specifying what the criteria are, these retailers attempt to control their costs. There is a down side to this tactic. These retailers are missing a golden opportunity to attract new customers to whom this type of program might appeal by not announcing it publicly.

Related to the free Thanksgiving turkey program is the free Easter ham program. Very similar in structure to the turkey programs, this program has been run with good results by a number of retailers around the United States.

Points Program

Points programs as addressed here are short-term, fixed-length promotions designed to skew customer spending using points rather than price.

There are numerous variations of these types of programs. All are based on customers accumulating a specified number of points during the promotion in order to earn a specified reward. These programs offer a great deal of flexibility to the retailer, in that they allow different promotions.

Bi-Lo, headquartered in Greenville, South Carolina, ran a points program in the following manner. Customers earned one point for each dollar spent. The customers could then use their accumulated points to "buy down" the retail price of selected feature items. For example, tuna might have been advertised at 49 cents, but customers could "buy down" the price to 19 cents with 50 points.

Gerland's Food Fair, based in Houston, Texas, has a different twist. In addition to earning one point for each dollar spent, customers can earn bonus points by purchasing selected products around the store. Gerland's uses this approach to promote the sale of their signature items, or private label products. Points are then redeemed for discount certificates.

Clubs

The most popular club programs seem to be baby clubs and pet clubs. These programs are designed to reward customers for their spending within a certain category.

Felpausch Food Centers runs a pet club, rewarding customers with a $10 gift certificate for every $100 they accumulate in pet category purchasing. Likewise, a number of retailers run baby clubs structured very similarly. These programs can be very effective in changing customer spending, but they must be promoted on a regular basis. In addition, they will work best in clearly defined categories; the customer must be able to understand which products count toward earning their rewards, and which don't. It is fairly easy for customers to understand what a baby or pet product is. In other categories, the definition can become somewhat blurred.

Build-upon Programs

In these programs, customers earn multiple rewards based on their spending during a specified program period. For example, customers spending $200-$399 earn a 5% discount certificate. Customers spending $400-$599 earn a $5 certificate plus the 5% certificate. Customers spending over $600 earn a 10% discount certificate, the $5 certificate, and the 5% certificate.

Continuity Programs

Many retailers run some type of continuity program during the year. Whether for dishes, cookware, or other merchandise, continuity programs tied to the retailer's frequent shopper card can be very powerful. Rather than ask customers to save stamps or collect receipts, base the continuity program on their spending, and track it electronically through their cards.

Green Hills Farms, in conjunction with The Continuity Company (London, UK) ran just such a program to test its effectiveness. Using a set of cookware as the reward, Green Hills created a four tier program allowing customers to qualify for discounts of 25%, 50%, 75%, or earning the entire set of cookware free, based upon the customer's spending during the 10 weeks of the program.

The results were impressive. At a time of great competitive activity, Green Hills was able to generate the highest number of $100+ per week average spending customers than at any time in its history. At the same time, customer retention improved, thus adding a secondary benefit to the program.

As Richard Beattie, Chief Executive of The Continuity Company, has stated to me, "We have been encouraging retailers for years to redirect some of their traditional markdown expense into funding a continuity program designed to encourage higher customer spending. But it has not been until the advent of frequent shopper cards, and the accompanying customer data, that we have been able to prove their worth to a retailer."

A continuity program, much as other types of reward programs, is simply a way for the retailer to begin altering the reward structure that they offer their customers. As with all such schemes, it is the perceived value of the reward that provides the incentive for customers to alter their shopping behavior in order to qualify for the reward.

The goal of all reward programs, as discussed here, should be to increase the number of higher spending customers in the retailer's customer base, improve customer retention, and to increase the inflow of new customers in to the retailers' stores.

In all marketing programs designed to increase customer spending, it is important that customers be able to easily check their status. Retailers use their communication vehicles to report back to customers their spending to date during a program by printing the status on the bottom of their receipts, through a kiosk, or through an interactive voice response system.

For example, during the continuity promotion at Green Hills as just mentioned, customers could check their spending total at kiosks located around the store to monitor their spending towards earning their rewards. One lady, finding she was $250 short of earning a free set of cookware the day before the promotion ended, did an extensive shop, spending over $300 to ensure that she received the cookware free!

Additionally, if using a points based program, consider how customers not only monitor their points balance, but how they redeem their points during the program.

There is an interesting phenomenon occurring around the world in regard to marketing programs such as the ones described here. The Hawthorne effect is a management term used to describe a change in behavior that occurs simply because the behavior is studied. Roethlisberger, a management consultant, first noted this when studying productivity in a factory setting; the term *Hawthorne effect* takes its name from the plant where the study took place. The workers improved their productivity simply because someone was measuring what they were doing.

Similarly, we see a Hawthorne-type effect when looking at marketing programs. The first time such a program is run typically produces far stronger results than subsequent efforts using the same program. Whether customers become bored with it, or for some other reason, the second or third time a similar program is run produces weaker results. Therefore, it is becoming a recommended practice to build a repertory of different programs that are run intermittently; the retailer can thus avoid running the same basic programs back-to-back.

Some of the do's and don'ts for running marketing programs:

Do:

- Run a program for a defined length of time. It does not matter if it is a 10-week or a 10-month program, as long as it does terminate at some time. Programs that are ongoing, at some point cease to provide an incentive to alter customer shopping behavior, and simply become an entitlement, increasing the cost structure of the retailer with no associated gain.

- Make it simple for the customer to understand. We prefer programs that are 10 weeks in length (easier for the customer to calculate the weekly average spending required) or calendar month, if possible.
- Make sure your information systems are accurate! You will be rewarding customers based on their shopping activity using their frequent shopper cards. Customers must be able to trust your information or you will be doing more harm than good.
- Make sure your store associates are well briefed on the program. Any associate in the store, but especially at the front end, should be able to communicate the program quickly and concisely to customers.

Don't:

- Don't make your program confusing. Once a program is designed, bounce it off some of your store-level people. Is it easy for them to understand? Does it make sense?
- Don't make your customers jump through hoops! While customers will respond to an incentive that makes sense, they do not like to be overtly manipulated.

Declining / Defecting Customers

Wouldn't it be wonderful if we could identify and retain those customers who are in the process of declining in their shopping with us or are ready to defect to a competitor? Many retailers we speak to around the world would like to make some effort to lure back those customers who have already left them.

This is a very challenging area. Quite honestly, we have not yet seen a defected customer program that offers a good return on investment. Any retailer can lure back a departed customer by making the reward rich enough. The challenge lies in keeping the customer coming back regularly without an expensive inducement.

Experience has shown that as retailers concentrate their efforts in managing their CCM scorecard — increasing the number of higher-spending customers, and recognizing and rewarding their existing customers — lower customer defection rates follow as a by-product. Rather than expending effort on customers who have already gone, devote your efforts and expenditures to your existing customers. They offer you a much better return on investment.

There is, however, an area in which defected customers can be of some value to a retailer. That is in the area of research. Consider doing an "exit interview" with Gold customers who have defected. Why have they gone? Did they move, or was there some problem with store operations? By doing this on a regular basis, a retailer can begin to discover problem areas within their operation.

It is also possible to learn other things. At one time, Green Hills made an effort to contact and bring back defected customers. We were contacting good customers who had stopped shopping for a period of several weeks. What we found was that we had a very large number of very good customers who went to Florida each winter for a period of several months. Even though we found these customers had not really defected, they very much appreciated our contacting them.

Services, Privileges, and Recognition

For a retailer to begin considering differentiating on services, privileges, and recognition some "out of the box" thinking is required. A majority of retailers consider adding services with the goal of drawing new customers or encouraging existing customers to spend more. No thought is given to using these services to differentiate between customers, or to measurably improve sales or customer retention. The new customer specific retail enterprise realizes that services are critically important in building relationship loyalty, and they work to integrate them into their daily operations, with the goal of targeting specific services to specific customers.

Recognition is an extremely powerful psychological force. Many successful business leaders recognize this and use it very effectively in their internal organizations. Management books have been devoted to recognition programs for company associates, such as recognition of an associate of the month, an annual sales award, etc. Parents know that recognition is powerful in teaching and raising children. Why should it not be equally effective with our customers?

Recognition can be as simple as a store's employees learning a customer's name and using it when the customer is in the store. Several POS systems now allow the retailer to display the customer's name when the frequent shopper card is scanned. Lees Supermarket in Westport, Massachusetts, was one of the first retailers to begin using this type of feature. The SASI eXPERIENCE POS system used by Green Hills greets the customer when his or her card is scanned, with a message displayed on the customer monitor. The customer's name is also displayed on the bottom of the cashier's monitor for the duration of the transaction, allowing the cashier to use the customer's name when speaking with him or her. Simple but effective.

It is becoming a common practice for retailers to provide their store managers with a list of the store's top customers on a regular basis, and suggest that the manager get to know these people by name. This can be particularly effective in building the type of relationship loyalty we are seeking. Who wouldn't frequent a store where the store manager knew you by name and greeted you every time you came in?

This practice can have some very interesting consequences. One retailer began supplying a list of the store's best customers to each of his store managers a few months after the launch of the frequent shopper card. One of the store managers discovered one day, when meeting his highest-spending customer, that it was the same person he yelled at occasionally for putting trash in the store's dumpster! It turns out the customer owned a tavern located near the store and was spending more than $400 a week purchasing snacks and other supplies!

Glen's Markets recognizes their best customers by sending birthday cards; wishing them a happy birthday and explaining that by bringing the card in to the store they will receive a free birthday cake. What a great way to recognize and reward your best customers!

Baker's in Omaha, Nebraska, held a special wine tasting party one evening at one of their upscale stores. A special invitation was sent to their top 100 customers, inviting them to attend this special wine tasting and meet the winemaker.

Green Hills was searching for a way to recognize our very best customers during the holiday season. We considered taking them to dinner somewhere, but then came up with the idea of holding a special holiday party right in the store. Invitations were sent to our top 200 customers — based on spending levels — inviting them and their spouses to a party at the store one night after Thanksgiving. The store was closed early that night, all the products moved out of the produce department, and a huge buffet table set up. The store was decorated for the holidays, and the management team was dressed in black tie. Customers were told the event was semiformal. The store was not open for business during this time, and nothing was sold that evening. This was simply a thank-you for some very special customers.

Of a potential 400 guests that evening, 200 came to the party. Customers were greeted at the door, where a coat check area was provided. As they came around the corner and saw the decorated produce department and the huge buffet table, you could see their jaws drop.

As I spoke with customers that evening, several very interesting things came out. Many people told me they just did not know what to expect — it was not every day that a supermarket invites their customers to a semiformal party! What was particularly fascinating were comments that night, and in the weeks following, about how customers appreciated the party as a time to get to meet us and speak with us. These people said that, although they often saw us (the managers) in the store, it always seemed that we (the managers) were too busy to talk with them (the customers). They really appreciated that evening as an opportunity to build a relationship with us.

When I relate this story, I am often asked how many customer complaints we had from closing the store early and doing something special for a small group of customers. The answer is two. The evening the store closed, I received a telephone call from an irate person who told me that what we were doing was illegal, and that our competitors would never do such a thing. The other comment was from a woman, in the store a couple of weeks later, who asked me what the party had been all about. Initially, she was not too happy about the store being closed, but as I explained what we did, and why, she became more understanding. All in all, this party was a fascinating exercise in customer recognition.

Some retailers are now extending differentiation into the areas of services and privileges. At Green Hills Farms, customer check cashing privileges are tied to customer loyalty. "Diamond" customers (highest-spending) have far greater check cashing privileges than "Opal" (lower-spending) customers. "Diamonds" can cash more checks, and for greater amounts, than "Opal" customers. Other retailers are also moving in this direction, either by using their POS systems to signal who the preferred customers are; or, in some cases, issuing "gold" cards to their best customers. Lees Supermarkets waives their check cashing fee for their best customers.

Customer service is another area where differentiation can be effective. Many retailers with customer databases have begun checking their data before responding to written customer comments. They respond to all, but respond differently based on their information.

At one time, Green Hills was between private label programs due to a change our wholesaler was making, and the store was quite low on private label products. One day, one of our cashiers told us that a customer had just come through her line who was very upset due to the lack of private label merchandise. Apparently, this woman had a large family and purchased private products for the savings they offered. She felt that she was being penalized by having to buy the national brands. She left the store very upset, but our cashier had obtained her name from her Green Hills card before she left. Looking this customer up in our database, we found that she was spending on average more than $200 a week with us, and that she had spent more than $17,000 in the past 18 months.

We certainly responded. I immediately called her on the telephone and explained our situation to her. After hanging up, I wrote a letter reaffirming our conversation and my explanation. Knowing the value of this customer, we included a $100 gift certificate with the letter, telling her that we hoped this made up for the extra she was spending buying the national brands. A few weeks later, when our new line came in, we made up a gift basket of assorted private label products and had it delivered to her front door. As John Mahar, Director of Green Hills Farms, would say, "All our customers are equal... some are just more equal than others!"

The opportunities to use customer information are limited only by the retailer's creativity. For example, on Labor Day weekend 1998, the Syracuse area was struck by a tornado which did a terrific amount of damage, including knocking out electric service to more than 300,000 households and most of the area's major supermarkets. A few days later, when people had their power restored, Green Hills sent out a letter to our "Diamond" customers, including a 10% discount certificate they could use when shopping to restock their refrigerators and freezers. Surprise rewards can be very powerful tools in increasing customer loyalty.

When in Australia presenting to a group of retailers, I had a fascinating discussion with the owner of a small chain of upscale women's shoe stores. He had been looking for a way to differentiate among his customers; lower prices or sales did not necessarily appeal to his upscale clientele. Finally, he had an idea. Each season, this retailer must review all the new shoe fashions coming out and decide which models to stock in his stores. Rather than making this decision alone, he thought of inviting his top customers to a private luncheon and shoe fashion show. There, the new fashions would be displayed and he would allow his best customers to pick which shoes his stores would carry. Brilliant!

Many retailers run customer focus groups. Think of running focus groups by customer category. For example, run a group made up of all Gold customers, and another made up of Tin customers, and then study their differences. Fascinating research.

Customer specific retailers will make this type of information available to their management teams, especially at the store level where this type of information can be most effective. As Tom Murphy, Vice President of Information Systems for Kroger, has said, "Making this information available to store-level associates lets even a large retailer treat their customers as the corner grocer once did." Use high tech to facilitate high touch.

Working and Shopping in the New Retail Enterprise

Chapter 11: Merchandising

Retailers now have the ability to look beyond product movement to see the customers behind it. Who is buying the products and what type of customers are they? The customer specific retail enterprise, being customer led, is interested in providing the products that their higher-spending, more profitable customers want, rather than simply moving a lot of product, but to the wrong customers.

We are seeing a great deal of interest recently among retailers with a frequent shopper program who want to link their customer data to their product data. This concept has created a buzz in the supermarket industry, but no concrete methods for accomplishing it. Most retailers are trying to use their top few deciles of customers as their best customers, and are looking at their product movement data. The problem is that a decile, as we saw in Chapter 5, is a moving target, hence not a stable platform to work from.

It is better to use our customer category management scorecard as the basis for our analysis, and then overlay this with product category data, creating a matrix. This is the process the larger companies — those with an established structure to support product category management — are pursuing. This matrix looks something like the one shown in Figure 11-1.

Customer Category Management/Product Category Management Matrix — By Households

	Customer Category				
Product Category	Gold	Silver	Bronze	Tin	Total
Carbonated Beverage	99%	96%	88%	52%	63%
Laundry Detergent (liquid)	90%	79%	58%	14%	29%

Of all households in a customer category, this report shows the percentage of total that are active in the specified product category. For example, 58% of all Bronze customers have purchased in the liquid laundry detergent category.

Customer Category Management/Product Category Management Matrix — By Sales

	Customer Category				
Product Category	Gold	Silver	Bronze	Tin	Total
Carbonated Beverage	20.3%	32.5%	20.4%	26.8%	100%
Laundry Detergent (liquid)	23.1%	35.6%	20.9%	20.4%	100%

Of the total product category sales, this report shows the sales divided over the customer categories. For example, of all carbonated beverage category sales, 32.5% came from Silver customers.

Gold Customers = $100 + SPW (Spending Per Week)
Silver Customers = $50 - $99.99 SPW
Bronze Customers = $25 - $49.99 SPW
Tin Customers = < $24.99 SPW

Data from "Schuyler" Markets, reporting period one quarter (12 weeks).

© 1999 DataWorks Marketing Group, LLC

Figure 11-1

We can now begin to see which of our categories are appealing to our higher-spending Gold customers, and which to our cherry pickers. For example, in Figure 11-1 we see that 99% of the Gold customers are shopping in the carbonated beverage category, while only 14% of the Tin households are active in the laundry detergent category.

This analysis alone can be eye-opening for many retailers, but we can go even further. Given the proper database and information systems, we do not have to be content with simply looking at the product category total; we can drill down to the actual brands within the category. Retailers can now see, for the first time, which specific brands appeal to which types of customers. Think of the implications of having this type of information available when putting together product category plans, shelf space plans, advertising plans, and looking at which products to discontinue.

In Figure 11-2 we take the categories shown in Figure 11-1 and drill down to the brand level. We now see that of the 90% of Gold customers shopping in the liquid laundry detergent category, almost 60% of them bought the Unilever product, versus only 38.7% purchasing the Procter & Gamble products.

Retailers can organize a product category based on their customer data. Which brands and sizes within the category most appeal to the higher-spending customers? Which brands and sizes most appeal to the lower-spending customers? By using this type of information, retailers can begin tailoring their stores to specific customer

CCM/PCM/Brand Level Matrix — By Households

	Customer Category				
Product Category	**Gold**	**Silver**	**Bronze**	**Tin**	**Total**
Carbonated Beverage	**99%**	**96%**	**88%**	**52%**	**63%**
•Pepsi	97.6%	90.6%	83.4%	69.3%	76.6%
•Coke	87.8%	79.6%	69.0%	49.6%	59.8%
•Other					
Laundry Detergent (liquid)	**90%**	**79%**	**58%**	**14%**	**29%**
•Procter & Gamble	38.7%	29.4%	25.1%	17.4%	25.0%
•Unilever	59.7%	51.3%	43.2%	39.5%	45.8%
•Other	51.6%	53.3%	52.7%	50.4%	52.0%

* Brand numbers are expressed as a percentage of the customer category active in the product category. For example, of the 58% of Bronze households active in the liquid laundry detergent category, 25.1% of them are purchasing the Procter & Gamble product.

Brand households within each customer category total more than 100% due to same households cross-purchasing, i.e., buying different brands within the reporting period.

CCM/PCM/Brand Level Matrix — By Sales

	Customer Category				
Product Category	**Gold**	**Silver**	**Bronze**	**Tin**	**Total**
Carbonated Beverage	**20%**	**33%**	**20%**	**27%**	**100%**
•Pepsi	57.2%	54.9%	54.1%	53.4%	54.8%
•Coke	36.4%	39.1%	39.4%	41.0%	39.2%
•Other	6.4%	6.0%	6.5%	5.6%	6.0%
Laundry Detergent (liquid)	**23%**	**36%**	**21%**	**20%**	**100%**
•Procter & Gamble	23.0%	18.8%	18.4%	14.9%	25.0%
•Unilever	35.3%	36.8%	39.5%	42.5%	45.8%
•Other	41.7%	44.4%	42.1%	42.6%	29.2%

* Brand numbers are expressed as a percentage of the customer category sales in the product category. For example, 33% of the carbonated beverage category sales come from the Silver customer category. Of that 33%, 54.9% are generated from Pepsi, 39.1% from Coke, and 6% from Other.

Gold Customers = $100 + SPW (Spending Per Week)
Silver Customers = $50 - $99.99 SPW
Bronze Customers = $25 - $49.99 SPW
Tin Customers = < $24.99 SPW

Data from "Schuyler" Markets, reporting period one quarter (12 weeks).

Figure 11-2

groups, especially to those customers who provide them with the majority of their profits.

Consider the ramifications to a retailer's advertising plans. The retailer now knows which specific products will most appeal to those customers they wish to attract; likewise, they now also know which items serve to attract the wrong type of customers, the unprofitable ones.

This is incredibly powerful information. Some time back I met with several brand managers from a very large consumer packaged goods company. These people were shocked that retailers could now have this level of information. They wanted to know how many retailers had this type of information, and how many of them understood it. The power within the retail industry is beginning to shift to the retail side...*for those who understand the power of their detailed customer information.*

Retailers can now begin to relate back to the manufacturers which brands and products they wish to advertise and promote. No longer will retailers write "blind" ads, knowing how many cases they may sell but not which types of customers may be buying them.

We can drill down even further, segmenting the brand customers by heavy, medium, or light buyers. Typically, this segmentation is done as follows: heavy buyers being the top 30% of customers (based on brand purchases); medium are the middle 40%, and light buyers are the bottom 30% of customers.

We have found it more helpful to use deciles when viewing brand purchases, rather than employing fixed spending thresholds, due to the great variance in spending by product categories. For example, in the soft drink category, a heavy buyer may spend $15-plus a week on soda purchases; whereas in the mustard category, $2 a week qualifies as a heavy buyer. Rather than try to develop benchmarks for each product category around the store, it is easier to work with the deciles used in these sample reports.

Perhaps as customer specific retailing evolves, we will develop fixed spending breaks by product category for this type of analysis. For the present, looking at the top 30%, middle 40%, and bottom 30% of a category or brand customers will be suitable for our purposes.

The report shown in Figure 11-3 drills down further into our customer information and provides an even more accurate picture of what is truly happening within our stores. It shows how relatively few customers are actually providing us, not only with our sales and profits, but also with the brand level sales.

The top report states information by households; the lower report, by sales. We can now see that the 2% of households that are Gold customers for the retailer and Pepsi "heavy" (top 30% in Pepsi purchasing) account for 13.7% of all Pepsi purchasing. Likewise, we see that "heavy" Pepsi households account for only 29.3% of the retailer's Gold customers, but they provide more than 65% of all Pepsi sales. All customers are not equal in their value to us...as retailers or as brands!

CCM/PCM/Brand Level Matrix — By Households

		Customer Category				
Product Category		**Gold**	**Silver**	**Bronze**	**Tin**	**Total**
Pepsi						
Heavy	Top 30%	2.0%	5.4%	5.7%	16.2%	29.3%
Medium	Middle 40%	2.7%	7.3%	8.0%	23.9%	41.9%
Light	Bottom 30%	2.1%	5.5%	6.1%	15.1%	28.8%
	Total	**6.8%**	**18.2%**	**19.8%**	**55.2%**	**100%**

For example, 2% of all customers purchasing Pepsi are Gold customers and also "heavy" Pepsi buyers.

Pepsi / heavy — the top 30% of customers by sales, purchasing Pepsi during report period.
Pepsi / medium — the middle 40% of customers by sales, purchasing Pepsi during report period.
Pepsi / light — the lowest 30% of customers by sales, purchasing Pepsi during report period.

CCM/PCM/Brand Level Matrix — By Sales

		Customer Category				
Product Category		**Gold**	**Silver**	**Bronze**	**Tin**	**Total**
Pepsi						
Heavy	Top 30%	13.7%	20.9%	13.3%	17.5%	65.4%
Medium	Middle 40%	6.3%	9.8%	5.7%	7.2%	29.0%
Light	Bottom 30%	1.2%	1.8%	1.2%	1.4%	5.6%
	Total	**21.2%**	**32.5%**	**20.2%**	**26.1%**	**100%**

For example, the 2% of all customers purchasing Pepsi are Gold. Gold/heavy Pepsi buyers generate 13.7% of all Pepsi sales.

Gold Customers = $100 + SPW (Spending Per Week)
Silver Customers = $50 - $99.99 SPW
Bronze Customers = $25 - $49.99 SPW
Tin Customers = < $24.99 SPW

Data from "Schuyler" Markets, reporting period one quarter (12 weeks).

Figure 11-3

Using this type of information, we can make more informed decisions about how to invest our marketing dollars. The customer specific retail enterprise does not have to offer the same deal to all customers. The retailer can invest its markdown expenditures with specific customers or customer groups, all with the goal of maximizing the return on investment.

There are many implications here for other segments of the retail industry, such as companies like IRI or Nielsen, that report product movement and market share data. For the customer specific retailer, it is less important what the total product movement is; it is much more important to know which customers are buying the product. The approach is customer focused, as opposed to product driven.

There are further complications with the traditional market share data that wholesalers and retailers have long utilized. What happens when retailers begin selling the same product at different prices to different customers? This can begin to invalidate market share data, which is based on sales. Retailers are already beginning to go to market this way, but we will be seeing an explosion in this area as more and more retailers bring their systems online to effectively and efficiently communicate and deliver customer specific offers.

The concept of basket analysis is similarly affected. Shopping basket analysis is inherently flawed, in that it is looking at the contents of an "average" basket, the items found in a majority of the shopping baskets. Some retail ers are attempting to take this information and utilize it in their merchandising plans and store layouts.

While there may be some value in doing this, the practice remains very difficult to measure properly. Not long ago I spent a day with the top management team of a large company that had just done some extensive basket analysis; over one million transactions were included in the study. There were some very interesting statistics that came out, but only after a fair amount of time spent simply trying to understand the information. After a time, I asked the grocery director what he would do with this information to improve the profitability of the company. No one in the room could specify a course of action; many of them conceded that while the information was interesting, it would be necessary to tie it to actual customer behavior to make it actionable.

There is no such thing as an average customer. No person likes to be thought of as "average." We are all individuals, each with our own desires, wants, and things that will motivate us. Customer specific retailers are shifting their perspectives viewing their stores from the inside out (products out to customers), to viewing them from the outside in. They are viewing their operations, advertising, store layouts, shelf sets, prices, etc., all from the customers' perspective. What will it take to maximize the spending, and lifetime value of each of our customers? And then how can we apply this to each individual customer?

This may be a good place to address product targeting. Many retailers begin frequent shopper programs with the intent of eventually targeting specific offers to their customers based on the customers' purchasing history. The problem is that this type of targeting becomes somewhat expensive to carry out; most retailers must still use direct mail to accomplish this. Mail can become very expensive when used on a regular basis.

Retailers many times look to their suppliers for assistance in their targeting efforts. They look to the vendor to support a targeted offer, by providing a "cents-off" for a certain product, as well as helping to offset the cost of the mailing piece. Vendors are usually willing to assist with these efforts, but in return they want to have some say as to who will be getting the offers.

It is typically an improved redemption rate on an offer that motivates both the retailer and the vendor to use this promotional tool. In the United States, the typical redemption rates for an FSI coupon are somewhere in the neighborhood of 2%. Depending on how the targeting is done, redemption rates of targeted offers can be much better than an FSI coupon; the averages we see around the United States are in the range of 4% to 12%. Certainly, very specific, rich, properly targeted offers can generate a much higher response rate, but these are more often the exception than the rule.

From the vendors' perspective, the goal is to move cases. They believe using a targeted offer may accomplish this by providing a reward to their existing customers, but also by providing an incentive for other customers buying in the category to purchase their product. It is here that the concept begins to deteriorate.

Just as the retailer must put value into their card programs to provide incentive to customers to use their card, so too must there be value in targeted offers for customers to make use of them. Customers do not find value in offers for products they are not interested in.

Some time ago, I was in Spain speaking at a conference. At dinner that evening, I sat next to a woman from the United Kingdom who shopped with one of the largest food retailers there and was a member of their loyalty program. As our conversation went on, she told me how she receives direct mail from the retailer on a regular basis, and that it typically contains targeted product offers. The problem, she said, was that the retailer was sending her offers for brands that she did not like. As she summed up her story, she told me, "Instead of them spending money to mail me offers for things I will not purchase, I wish they would simply send me a £2.50 or £5 discount certificate and let me buy the products I want!"

Retailers have also found that product targeting is very labor- and time-intensive using the present database tools. Indeed, the number of retailers doing product targeting declines each year, according to a survey done by one of the database companies.

Experience to date shows that focusing on increasing a customer's total spending, regardless of what specific products are bought, offers the highest return on investment for the retailer.

There are profound implications for the consumer packaged goods companies in the new retail enterprise. As more and more retailers develop the communication and delivery infrastructure for true one-to-one retailing (and remember, this technology is here today!), and develop a greater understanding of their customers, they will increasingly control their destinies. In essence, the retailers will now "own" the customer relationship.

It will be the continued development of customer specific retailing that will enable true, efficient consumer response. In fact, true one-to-one marketing is simply the natural evolution of this industry initiative to make the distribution and marketing of products more efficient and cost-effective. Just as retailers have now found that providing different rewards to different customers offers a much higher return on investment, so too will manufacturers find the same with regard to their advertising and promotional monies. Paying a retailer's fee for a front page ad placement, or a fee for an end cap display is no longer the most efficient use of their dollars. The game is changing.

Andersen Consulting, in their study entitled *The Daunting Dilemma of Trade Promotion,* found that the cost of trade promotion in the grocery products industry is in excess of $30-33 billion! In addition, hidden costs of another $5-8 billion are associated with the supply chain volatility and administration caused by this trade promotion.

Store exit interviews carried out by Andersen show that while promotions can generate incremental purchases, a significant number of people would have bought the item anyway or would have purchased their brand at full price.

Consumer Research Findings

- 60% of consumers said that promotions have no influence on store selection.
- Fewer than 30% of consumers look at weekly ads before shopping.
- Furthermore, a large portion of the sale items were given away. Consumers were unaware that 51% of all promoted items purchased were on sale — they received a discount that had no effect on their buying behavior.
- Of those "aware" of the promotion (49%):
  —40% would have bought the item anyway.
  —37% switched from another brand.
  —Only 23% purchased product incremental to their regular purchase behavior.

Andersen Consulting
The Daunting Dilemma of Trade Promotion

Until now, manufacturers have operated blindly with regard to their promotional monies; that is, they would give monies to a retailer to use in promotion of their product, but there was no way to measure results, other than by case movement. The Efficient Consumer Response movement within the supermarket industry recognizes the inefficiency of this system and attempts to streamline the trade dollars used in promotion. But only now, through the detailed customer information leading retailers have, can the effectiveness of promotions be measured by *individual customer.*

We can now apply many of the same principles and concepts of customer specific retailing to brand marketing. And, just as with retailers, we can now for the first time truly measure, by specific customer, customer shopping behavior with regard to brands.

Retailers who have the proper databases can now create a customer life cycle matrix for specific categories and brands within their stores. We can now identify which customers are new to a category or specific brand, which are existing customers, and which customers are defecting (moving to purchasing different brands).

As we saw at the retail level, we can now develop different marketing tactics and strategies based on these different customer segments. The challenge lies in bringing together both the manufacturers and the retailers to create a mutual win, ideally a win-win-win (manufacturer, retailer, and customer) scenario.

There certainly are opportunities for retailers and manufacturers to work together, but this must be done with eyes wide open, understanding that the basic agendas of each party are different.

As Figure 11-4 shows, customers can be loyal to a particular retailer, and yet be either loyal or promiscuous regarding brands of products they purchase from that retailer. Likewise, customers can be retailer-promiscuous, shopping many different stores, and yet be brand-loyal-purchasers, for example, buying Pepsi in each store. Given this situation, there is an opportunity to create joint marketing programs that focus on that segment of customers who are loyal to both the retailer and to the manufacturer's brand(s).

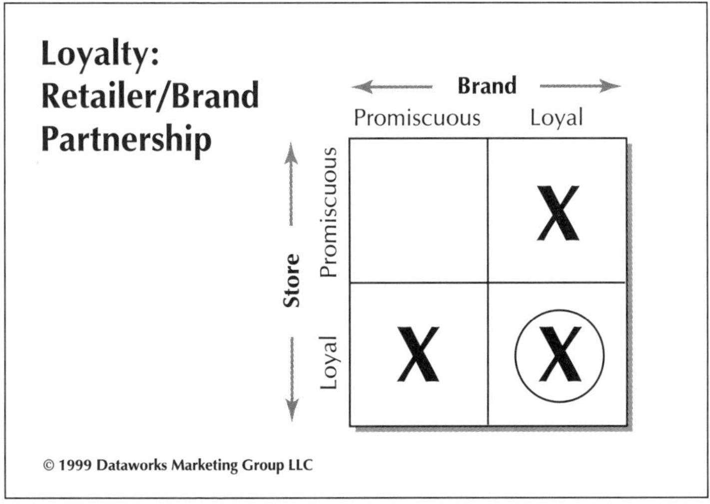

Figure 11-4

As an example, Green Hills Farms and Pepsi ran a joint promotion with this concept in mind. The program was managed through the Green Hills card, with the database used to track customer purchasing and issue the rewards. The "I Prefer Pepsi" program was three months long, and rewarded customers for their Pepsi purchases with free Pepsi product. Specifically, for every $25 customers spent on Pepsi products, they would receive a free six-pack of Pepsi (their choice of size and type). Customers spending $250 during the program would, in addition, receive a cooler filled with Pepsi products and a Pepsi t-shirt.

Pepsi in this case was looking to win by increasing case movement with a profitable sales gain, without resorting to massive price reductions. The retailer, Green Hills, was looking to improve retention of customers (the customers had to buy their Pepsi product at Green Hills to qualify for the rewards) and also to drive sales in the category.

The results of this program were substantial. Pepsi increased its share of category during the three-month program period by more than 9% from the same three-month period the previous year. The company realized a very strong increase in case movement and in sales, and was able to accomplish this with less price reduction than in the past.

Green Hills experienced a noticeable increase in customer retention in the soft drink category, and a very significant increase in overall category sales. This is a very good example of a retailer and manufacturer partnering together to create a true win-win-win scenario. The customer also wins in this type of promotion by receiving more value through altering his or her shopping behavior.

This effort reinforces one of the basic premises of customer specific marketing: it is much more profitable to encourage the already higher-spending customers to do even more shopping with the retailer than to try and convert the cherry pickers. The same concept also applies to the marketing of brands, though most manufacturers do not go to market this way. As with retailers of the past, manufacturers could not measure true customer shopping behavior; when looking at customer behavior with regard to brand loyalty, there are many surprises. It appears that there may be much less true brand loyalty than most manufacturers realize.

For example, one retailer found some shocking information when looking at his liquid laundry detergent category. Of customers purchasing a specific brand of liquid laundry detergent for the first time, only 5% of them purchased the same brand again in the succeeding 12 weeks. The other 95% of customers continued to purchase in the category, but purchased other brands.

Another retailer found that 67% of their highest spending customers exhibited great loyalty to one particular brand of butter. Which brand of butter do you think this retailer preferred to promote? This same retailer found a different story in the shredded cheese category. There, more than 80% of customers purchasing the leading brand defected to other brands within the category in the succeeding weeks.

There are tremendous opportunities for retailers and manufacturers to work together in building their mutual businesses, if they are willing to see what the data is telling them. Brand marketers must be aware of how the landscape is changing with regard to the information now available and the new communication and delivery tools being used.

Retailers who have and understand this level of customer information are in a very strong position. Retailers who can combine this understanding with a willingness to go to market differently, and who have the technology to practice customer specific retailing, are not as reliant on the manufacturers. The packaged goods companies now must bring to the table new value for the retailer in order to enhance their partnership. Can their products draw the customers the retailer wants? Can their brands be used to drive category sales and profits? These are all things that can now be measured, using the detailed customer information the retailer owns.

In the customer specific retail enterprise, the value of individual brands lies in using them to attract individual customers to whom the specific brands are of value. This implies making offers to different customers, using different brands from within the same category, at the same time.

There are also vast opportunities for combining detailed customer information with private label programs for those retailers committed to private label. As we saw previously, retailers can now do an analysis of their private label products across customer categories to see if indeed they are appealing to the customers who are most valuable to the retailer.

The promotional activities now available to the customer specific retailer are almost endless.

Tom Stephens, President of Brand Strategy of Toronto, Canada, suggests that retailers now provide free samples of a certain new private label product to the heaviest buyers in that category, rather than simply price promote it to all. Research has shown that within any given category, it is a relative handful of customers who generate the majority of the sales and case movement. The idea here is to get a free sample of the product into the hands of these people, encouraging some of them to switch. This promises a much better return on investment than past price promotions were able to offer.

In addition, Stephens also suggests involving the best customers in the actual selection of the final product to be put under private label. For example, a retailer creating a new private label cooking sauce may get the final decision down to three different formulas. At this point, the retailer could bring in the top 10 cooking sauce customers to let them sample the products and make the final decision. Incredible opportunities for marketing and promotion are suggested by this type of strategy.

It is also possible to tie private label products into a retailer's marketing programs. Some time back, Green Hills was approached to donate to a community playground project. Rather than write a check as we would have done in the past, we wanted to tie together the donation with our card program and our private label program. We created a three-month marketing program that would "donate" to the project 5% of all private label sales during the program. Customers would have to use their Green Hills cards each time they shopped, as this was how we tracked the sales of the private label.

This program resulted in an increase of 17% in the sales of private label product during the three-month promotion; and the store retained an increase of 10% in private label sales in the time after the promotion. In addition, there was an increase of 10% in the number of customer households purchasing private label.

There is a great deal of synergy in combining a strong frequent shopper program with a strong private label program, for those retailers who understand both.

The customer specific retailer is basing merchandising decisions on customer data. No longer is the retailer product driven. It is much more profitable for retailers to advertise and have on the shelf the products their more valuable customers are looking for.

To operate this way, the new retail enterprise constructs its information systems around its customer data. No longer are its product information systems separate from its customer data; they are integrated, and all data flows from the same central data bank. Product category managers need access to the customer data to make proper merchandising decisions; and customer managers need access to product data for use in their customer specific marketing efforts.

Working and Shopping in the New Retail Enterprise

Chapter 12: Countering Competitors

The new retail enterprise does not operate in a vacuum. At some point, all retailers face new competitors moving into their markets or old competitors remodeling old stores or opening new stores. The customer specific retailer has a valuable new weapon, however, that can significantly alter the field of battle: detailed customer information.

> *"Now an army may be likened to water, for just as flowing water avoids the heights and hastens to the lowlands, so an army avoids strength and strikes at weakness."*
>
> Sun Tzu

No longer do retailers have to fight fire with fire; they do not have to offer lower prices to compete with a new competitor's grand opening ads, which are typically packed with low-cost specials. The new retail enterprise can shift the field of battle, many times without the competitor even realizing what is happening.

Rather than fighting on a broad front, the customer specific retailer can narrow their efforts to retaining their best customers, who are supplying the majority of their sales and profits. By focusing their efforts in this way, the new retail enterprise can show a much better return on investment in the fight to retain business.

I wish to stress here that a frequent shopper card program, even a world-class program, is not a silver bullet — it is not a miracle worker. It is important for the retailer to employ competitive strategies to remain in the ball game. Clean floors, product on the shelf, good customer service, and all the other things that characterize a good retail operation are important for any company.

One medium sized chain had kicked off their card program, had begun differentiating, and was realizing some gross profit margin gains. When Wal-Mart opened several supercenters in town, this supermarket retailer didn't react. They were lulled by their early successes; they thought their card program would insulate them from this competition. They thought Wal-Mart would only take substantial business away from their competitors.

When Wal-Mart came to town, it lowered the retail price structure of the entire market. All the other supermarkets fought back by lowering their prices. This company with the card program simply sat back — and then awoke one day to find it had lost a major portion of its volume. The market had moved, and this company was no longer playing in the same ball game.

What good is intelligence during war if the generals do not understand the information and are not willing to make use of it? In the new retail wars, a piece of plastic in and of itself does not a competitive strategy make. The edge gained through a frequent shopper program is only as good as the retailer's understanding and willingness to use the data the program provides.

For those retailers whose physical plant, operations, and pricing do permit them to play in the same game as their competitors, the detailed customer information they obtain through their frequent shopper programs affords them great advantage. These retailers can now identify and concentrate on retaining their higher-spending, more profitable customers.

There are a number of different strategies for accomplishing this. Leading retailers, knowing a new competitor is opening near them, will launch some type of reward program prior to the competitive opening, thus helping retain their better customers with a rich reward. We cannot stop our customers from going to a competitor's store, but we can provide strong incentive to discourage them from spending much while there.

This is an area in which developing relationship loyalty among their customers can be invaluable to the new retail enterprise. As retailers tie their customers to them by using recognition, special customer services, and privileges, they begin to offer much better insulation against pure price competition. Though I regularly receive bonus miles offers from other airlines, I am reluctant to divert much of my travel from USAirways. This is because I value the recognition, services, and privileges they extend to me and I wish to retain them.

The new retail enterprise can measure and identify those customers they do lose to competitors, and can choose to contact them to try to bring them back. Again, it is important to focus resources on the more valuable lost customers rather than just anyone. And, there may be more value derived from contacting these lost customers in discovering why they left than in spending a great deal to bring them back.

Let's use Green Hills Farms as an example here. Green Hills was faced with not one, but two new competitors opening very nearby. Save-A-Lot was opening in the plaza across the street, while Aldi was opening a store just down the street. As it turns out, the new stores opened within a day of each other.

Knowing that these stores were moving into the market, Green Hills developed strategies to combat them. What made this even more interesting was that both these operators are low cost competitors; both have built their market niche on very low prices. It is difficult, if not impossible, for a conventional supermarket to compete with them on price. There were fears among store personnel and other observers that Green Hills could lose up to 25% of its sales volume to these new stores.

John Mahar, Director of Green Hills, talked with many other retailers around the country who also had to compete with these stores. The majority of these retailers had responded by bringing in additional, low price point, private label products, with the intention of competing with Save-A-Lot and Aldi on their own turf. Many times this tactic had only mediocre results. Mahar realized that it would take a different strategy to compete without losing any sales volume.

Green Hills found through their customer information that their customers preferred brand name products to more generic, low-price products. Mahar, armed with this information, decided to bring the battle to his turf by fighting these competitors with name brand products at low prices, rather than off-label products. His thinking was simple: given a choice between an off-label can of vegetables and a national name brand at the same price, which would customers respond to? Certainly Green Hills did not lower their everyday shelf prices to match the competitors' prices, but Mahar analyzed which products both competitors typically promoted. With this information, he then worked deals with suppliers to allow Green Hills to promote the brand name equivalent products at prices at or below the competitors'. For example, Save-A-Lot would promote two-liter soda at 59 cents; Mahar, working with Pepsi, would promote two-liter Pepsi at the same price.

This was the strategy Green Hills employed above the surface — what the public saw in their advertisements. There was also another strategy developed and employed below the surface, out of sight of the competitors. This was a strategy built on the detailed customer information gathered through the frequent shopper program.

Lisa Piron, Director of Information Systems for Green Hills, developed a list of the best customers by department within the store, as well as a list of the overall best store customers. These customers were identified as generating a great deal of the sales volume within each of the primary departments, as well as for the entire store.

A direct mail piece was designed — a letter thanking these people for being best customers. Included in the letter was a gift certificate, which the customer could bring in to the store to receive a free gift. Customers were instructed to stop by the customer service desk to receive their gifts. At the service desk, customers presented their certificates, and depending on which department was involved, the department manager was paged. This was an opportunity for the department manager to meet his or her best customers, thank them for their business, and personally give them their gifts.

Included in the direct mail piece were other discount certificates, good for a discount on purchases made within that department. For example, the best meat department customers received discounts for meat department purchases. It was explained to the customers in the letter that they could either use these discounts themselves, or give them as gifts to their friends, so they could also enjoy the products these customers valued. It was surprising how many of the certificates were used by other people.

The end result: rather than losing business, Green Hills actually gained. The two competitors opened within a day of each other. Green Hills increased business by feeding off the traffic flow of these competitors. In addition, the store experienced an increase in the number of new customers who joined the store's frequent shopper program, and was able to retain a number of these new customers over time. Green Hills, through its use of information, became the primary store, while customers cherry picked the two new competitors.

Another leading retailer used a different tactic. During this time period, the retailer was running a 5% program; customers would earn a 5% discount certificate for achieving certain spending thresholds during the program period. When this retailer saw that they had new competitors opening near several of their stores, they used this information to make a competitive move. They told their customers that during the competitors' grand opening week, their 5% discount certificates would be worth 20%. If the customers redeemed the certificates they were immediately awarded an additional 5% discount certificate.

Countering competitors is yet another area in which we can use customer category management to great advantage. Through this measurement, retailers can identify those households that are providing them with the majority of their sales and profits, and focus retention strategies on them. Likewise, it provides the scorecard for measuring the impact of the competitor on the customer specific retailer's business. Losing sales from cherry pickers is much less painful than losing sales from higher-spending customers.

One regional retailer, when faced with a competitive challenge, responded with traditional tactics, lowering prices and making their advertised specials even more aggressive. They were able to maintain sales volume, but at a cost. It became evident, when looking at its customer information, that they were losing their high-spending customers and replacing them with cherry pickers. It was only by using the customer category management scorecard that these changes were observable and measurable.

As in battle, when the weapons change, the strategies and tactics must change. Retailers armed with detailed customer information have new firepower with which they can change the rules of engagement.

> *"Those skilled in war bring the enemy to the field of battle and are not brought there by him."*
>
> Sun Tzu

Working and Shopping in the New Retail Enterprise

Chapter 13: Management Practices

In order for something to be managed, it must first be measured. For decades, mass merchandising retail has been managed by measuring product data and the company's expenses. Much of what is reflected in a retailer's financial statements flows from product measurements: sales, inventory levels, gross profit margins, and so on. In addition, retailers have become masters of controlling their own expenditures, such as labor expense, rent factors, utilities, etc. Never during the past sixty years have there been customer measures.

Yes, many retailers track the number of transactions they have each week or each quarter. But this is not the same as true customer tracking. Some of our customers shop only once every 10 weeks, others several times a week. They each count as one transaction each time they shop, but we have had no way of knowing who was who, i.e., which of our customers were more valuable to us.

At the end of the day, a business is managed by its financial statements. This is the information that companies, literally, live and die by. The customer specific retailer has reworked their financial statements to include measurements of customer behavior.

In Chapter 8, "New Metrics and Economics," we discussed how some retailers are now reporting their markdown expense on their profit and loss statements. These companies are now reporting sales at full margin and expensing the cost of their price reductions. Since this expense is now included in their financial statements, by nature it is accorded much more attention than before, when it was an "off financial statement" number.

Let's take this a step further. One of the reasons companies would want to expense their markdown cost is to make it more visible, allowing for better overall management. The other reason, most important to the customer specific retailer, is so that the markdown expense is allocated across the different customer categories, thus ensuring it is being monitored to provide the best return on investment.

Rather than simply reporting top line sales, the customer specific retailer is now reporting total sales by customer category. It is important to these retailers to know the composition of their customer base; changes in the customer base directly affect profit margins, due to the varying levels of profitability offered by different customers.

This use of customer categories for reporting sales is applicable to total company sales, individual store level sales, and department level sales. The same principles and concepts that have been discussed here for a retailer are equally applicable to individual departments within the store.

One of the goals of the "information revolution" is to make more and more information available to our company associates at a deeper and deeper level. The more information our front line people have with which to make decisions, the better they will be able to do their jobs.

Why not provide this type of customer information to the managers of the cosmetic department or the produce department? They are responsible for the sales and profits of their respective areas — would they not be much more effective if they had customer information?

Customer specific retailers are still comparing their performance year-to-year, but are using the new metrics to do so. Are they increasing the number of "gold" customers as a proportion of their total customer base year-to-year? Are they improving their retention rate of "bronze" customers year-to-year? This is an entirely different way to view our retail businesses, and it is exceptionally powerful.

In addition to reporting product inventories, inventory turns, and inventory shrink, the customer specific retailer can now report customer inventory, customer turns, and customer shrink. Just as managers have for years managed their product inventory, we can now manage our customer base.

For the customer specific retailer, product no longer has center stage. These retailers are organizing their entire businesses around customer information. It logically follows that their reporting and measurement systems will contain customer information more prominently than product information.

Many retailers have some type of incentive and bonus system in place to encourage the behavior and results they want from their associates. Now that we have new measurements of our customer behavior, why not change the incentives to encourage the behavior we are after: *higher-spending, more loyal customers.*

How can this work? One well-known retailer has already moved to tying 50% of their store directors' bonuses to these new measures. These store directors are now held accountable for the number of "gold" customers they have each period, and the retention of them. Basic psychology: reward the behavior you seek.

This same incentive system is equally applicable at the department level. Many retailers provide some type of bonus to their department level managers for achieving certain performance levels, typically tied to sales, profit margins, and inventory levels. Again, with our new information, these targets can be changed to include customer based metrics.

Let's take this in the other direction — up. Why couldn't boards of directors hold their top management teams responsible for these new metrics? First and foremost would be their identification levels — the percentage of total sales and transactions captured. Without this foundation, none of the rest of this philosophy is possible. Retailers maintaining the highest identification rates have owners and top management teams who are fully committed to this new way of going to market.

Almost any retailer, of any size, will say that customer service and creating loyal customers is a key part of their company mission. We can now quantify and measure customer loyalty. Why not hold top management responsible for customer retention? And for the number of higher-spending customers the company has?

Larger retailers have long measured their share of market. This has been one of their critical measures of success, being able to maintain and grow their market share. The inherent problem is that today's markets are changing very quickly. We need look no further than the retailing of books. What good is market share when an Internet-based retailer like Amazon.com comes in and within a very short period of time does more in sales than some of the largest store-based book retailers? The world is changing much too quickly to be tied to fixed ideas of markets.

The one constant in today's world is customers. The customer specific retailer is more concerned with share of customer than with share of market.

Traditional supermarket retailers are faced with declining market shares because they are now confronting many non-traditional competitors. Supermarkets are being hit from all sides, with Wal-Mart on one side and new food providers such as Eatzi's or Boston Market on the other. What good is a share of market measurement of traditional supermarket retail? Having a larger share of a continuously shrinking market is not a viable, long-term business plan.

The world of retail revolves around customers. They are the one constant in this ever-changing world. The new retail enterprise recognizes this, and has built its systems around the gathering, understanding, and use of detailed customer information. The customer specific retailer is continuously morphing their business with the goal of constantly maximizing the lifetime value of their customer base by growing their share of customer.

Section 5: Where to Next?

Lest anyone reading this book think that customer specific retailing as presented here is science fiction, I want to assure you that the systems and processes described here are, in fact, in use.

It is not technology that is holding back the growth of the new retail enterprise. Many companies already have many of the necessary technologies in place. It is a lack of understanding of their customer information that is impeding many retailers from moving to the next stage in the evolution to true customer specific retailing.

An additional impediment is resistance to change. It is difficult for many retailers to overcome decades of product based, mass merchandise retailing.

Will customer specific retailing win out? Will it supplant the more traditional forms of product based retailing? Only time will tell.

Certainly the economics are very powerful. When looking over the course of history, one sees that only rarely has a superior economic model failed to eventually overcome less efficient models. We need look no further than the historical battle between free market economics and the state directed economy, as evidenced by the United States and the former Soviet Union.

Indeed, when looking throughout the history of mankind, we see strong evidence that economics has been a powerful motivating force. A strong case can be made that conflicts ranging from the Crusades to the Civil War to the more recent battles in the Middle East were all motivated by economic issues.

The customer specific retail enterprise is built on a new economic model, one that offers a better profit yield than the product based retail model of old. Try taking it away from the retailers who are experiencing substantial profit gains. For them, there is no going back.

Where to Next?

Chapter 14: Customer Specific Retailing

We have now set the stage for true customer specific retailing. It is now possible, using all the information gathered, to begin learning what motivates our customers to shop the way they do. Using this knowledge, we can begin grading our customers on their loyalty quotient, all with the goal of maximizing our customers' lifetime value.

Before going further, we need to define what loyalty is. There are basically two types of loyalty: economic loyalty and relationship loyalty. Economic loyalty is loyalty which is simply deal-driven; this is essentially loyalty which you "buy" on a temporary basis with a certain deal. Relationship loyalty in the retail field is defined as customers shopping with a retailer for reasons other than financial motivation. Perhaps their cousin works at the store, or they prefer the retailer's butcher shop.

Examples of economic loyalty are all around us. A couple of years ago, McDonald's ran a promotion in which they gave away a beanie baby stuffed toy with each Kid's Meal purchased. Now, I have never been a frequent visitor to

McDonald's, but a couple of my children were crazy about beanie babies at the time. During a weekend ski trip to Vermont we must have stopped at six McDonald's, simply to get their beanie babies! For that weekend, I was a loyal, high-spending McDonald's customer. But when the promotion ended and our weekend trip was over, I disappeared from their radar screens. Economic loyalty.

Compare this with an example of relationship loyalty. I am a frequent traveler, accumulating more than 100,000 miles with USAirways each year. I am at the highest level of their frequent flier program. When I first began traveling, I began centralizing my travel on USAirways to get upgrades and free travel. Over time, I achieved the highest level in their program and was accorded certain services and privileges. Each time I make a reservation, I am automatically upgraded to First Class. The airline attendants greet me by name. One time, I was traveling to Chicago and had to transfer in Pittsburgh. I got on the flight for Chicago, but after some time the flight was cancelled due to bad weather. As I was exiting the plane, a USAirways person pulled me aside, apologized for the problem, and informed me that they had booked me on the next flight to Chicago, due to leave in a couple of hours. I explained that this would cause me to miss my meeting in Chicago and asked them to return me to Syracuse. They booked me on the next flight home, gave me a voucher for a free lunch in the airport, and refunded the entire cost of my air travel that day. That is service, and that engenders relationship loyalty.

One lesson to keep in mind is that we need to look beyond the absolute numbers and measurements that are now available to us to see what the numbers tell us about our customers. By measuring not only what a customer spends, but also the amount of markdown he or she receives, we can begin to discover what motivates that customer. For example, a customer spending $100 a week but receiving $20 a week in markdown is more motivated by price and deals than another customer who may also spend $100 a week, but receive only minimal markdown. This is a customer shopping for other reasons; deals are not as important to this customer. This customer is driven more by relationship loyalty.

What do we do with this information? We begin building a profile of our customers. We can now measure a customer's purchasing, and as such, an idea of his or her loyalty. We can also begin to measure a customer's loyalty to product categories and specific brands around the store. The idea here is to identify which categories and specific products may motivate that customer to shop with us. Lastly, we can begin to develop a measure of a customer's deal loyalty/relationship loyalty ratio. All this information is required to practice true customer specific retailing.

The goal of all this is to provide a true customer specific retail shopping experience — providing a mix of products, prices, services, privileges, and information to each individual customer that is designed to maximize his or her lifetime value to the retailer. A retailer should try to

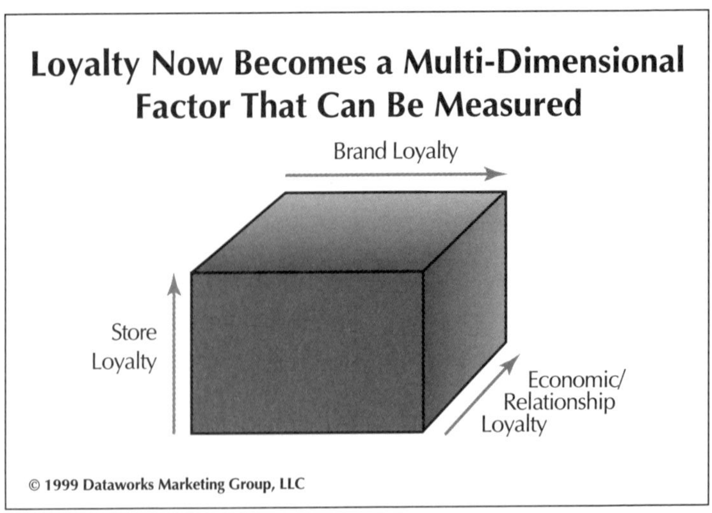

Figure 14-1

build relationship loyalty with customers, rather than simple deal loyalty. Relationship loyalty is more profitable to the retailer; deal driven customers will simply rush off to the next retailer who offers a richer loyalty scheme.

The first step in this evolution to advanced customer specific retailing is a further segmentation of our customer base using the CCM scorecard. Since higher-spending customers are more profitable, and spending is an indication of loyalty to a particular retailer, it is by itself an indicative measure of customer behavior. By measuring not only the purchases of our customers, but also what they are receiving in markdown, we can develop the type of report shown in Figure 14-2.

We can now see by customer category whether our customers are more deal driven or relationship motivated.

Customer Category Management

Deal Loyalty / Relationship Loyalty Analysis

Loyalty Type			Gold	Silver	Bronze	Tin
Relationship	(Lowest 20%)	1	19	112	155	796
	Markdown Expense By Quintile	2	19	111	155	796
		3	18	111	154	796
		4	18	111	154	796
Deal	(Highest 20%)	5	18	111	154	796
	Total Category:		92	556	772	3980

Figure 14-2

This knowledge is then used in deciding how we go to market. Remember, we can now communicate and deliver customer specific offers to our customers. Essentially we are devising a separate marketing strategy for each customer segment, in an attempt to improve the lifetime value of our customers.

For example, in Figure 14-2, we can see that of the Gold customers, 19 are relationship driven, 55 are split between deal and relationship, and 18 are very strongly deal driven. The goals of the retailer are now to increase the spending and retention of all these Gold customers, and to try to move as many customers as possible over into the relationship category.

American Express Platinum cardholders are not deal driven people; they are motivated by the services and prestige offered by the Platinum card. American Express does a wonderful job of identifying people who hold an American Express Green card and moving them up to the Gold card, and eventually to the Platinum card level. At each stage, American Express ties in more services and benefits to offset the higher annual cost to the cardholder. In the course of using these services, the customer uses his or her AmEx card that much more, thus becoming a more profitable customer for American Express. For example, as a Platinum cardholder, I can call a special telephone number for dinner reservations at a number of the most popular restaurants in major cities around the United States. When using this service, what card do you think I use when it's time to pay the bill?

A retailer can now begin to selectively offer enhanced services and recognition to those customers who warrant it and whom it will motivate. For example, the retailer may offer a special shopping service only to selected Gold customers to whom such a service would appeal.

With the proper information systems, we can begin identifying specific products that are important to each of our customers. Once these items are identified, the retailer can begin offering these products to the customer on a regular basis (with the offers tied to the rate of product use), thus encouraging the customer to shop with the retailer.

We can now tie this all together by creating an individual "virtual" scorecard for each of our customers. The scorecard could look something like the one shown in Figure 14-3.

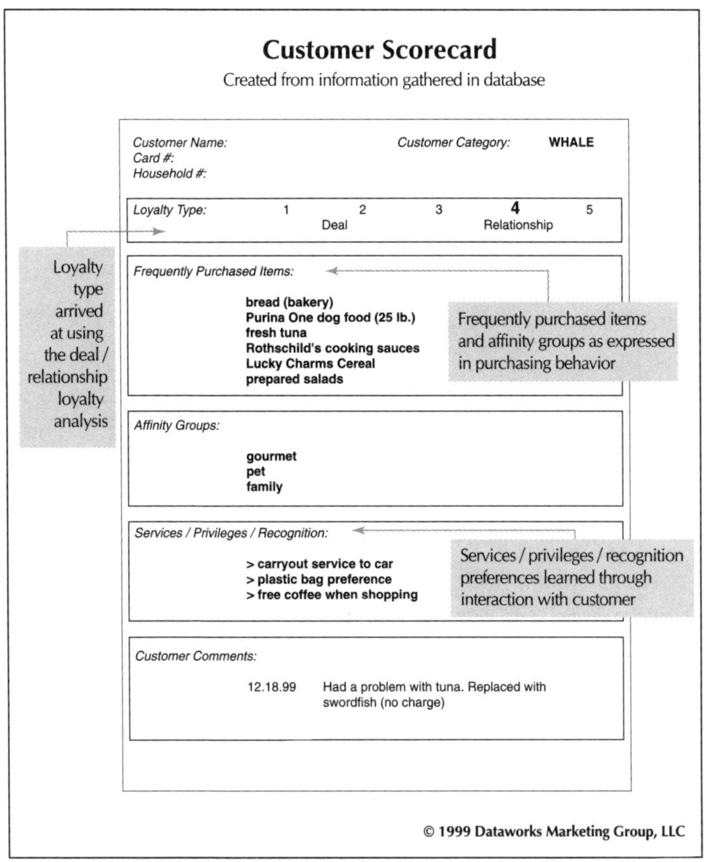

Customer Scorecard

Created from information gathered in database

Customer Name:
Card #:
Household #:

Customer Category: **WHALE**

Loyalty Type: 1 2 3 **4** 5
Deal Relationship

Loyalty type arrived at using the deal / relationship loyalty analysis

Frequently Purchased Items:

bread (bakery)
Purina One dog food (25 lb.)
fresh tuna
Rothschild's cooking sauces
Lucky Charms Cereal
prepared salads

Frequently purchased items and affinity groups as expressed in purchasing behavior

Affinity Groups:

gourmet
pet
family

Services / Privileges / Recognition:

> carryout service to car
> plastic bag preference
> free coffee when shopping

Services / privileges / recognition preferences learned through interaction with customer

Customer Comments:

12.18.99 Had a problem with tuna. Replaced with swordfish (no charge)

Figure 14-3

This now serves as the basis for our marketing to individual customers.

It is computers that give retailers the capability to do this type of thing on a mass basis. In a sense, we are practicing mass customization as presented in the book *Mass Customization — The New Frontier in Business*

Competition by B. Joseph Pine II. The technology for doing this exists today, but it takes a great deal of customer information and learning on the part of the retailer to put it all together.

It is only by running different types of marketing programs, or by offering different types of services that a retailer can learn what is important to individual customers. For example, a retailer may provide its "gold" customers with a free cup of coffee any time they are shopping. Simply by looking at who took advantage of the offer, we can learn to whom it is important, and who would value this type of offer in the future.

We can also begin to append to our customer information a customer comment database. American Express is a master at this, maintaining a record of each interaction with the customer, so that no matter who speaks with that customer next, he or she will know the complete history of interaction with that specific customer. Think of the implications of this at store level. A store manager would be able to know that the customer with whom she is speaking, is a "gold" level customer and had a problem with a package of meat bought the previous week, for example.

Edward Deming is perhaps the "father" of the Total Quality Management movement in the United States and certainly in Japan, where he helped Japanese industry thrive in the aftermath of World War II. Some years ago, prior to his death, I had the opportunity to attend one of Deming's famous four-day seminars, where he taught the principles of total quality management. One of the key concepts presented was a process improvement cycle.

This cycle shows the learning steps involved when breaking a process down to its component parts. For example, a manufacturer will analyze a production process, discover an opportunity to improve a part of the process, implement the change, study the results, and apply more changes — all as part of a never ending cycle toward improving quality and lowering the waste or shrink.

Customer specific retail enterprises are modifying Deming's process improvement cycle and applying it to their process of learning why their customers shop the way they do. They run a program (or process), learn from it, and then reapply the learning to make the process more efficient, less wasteful, and, hence, more profitable.

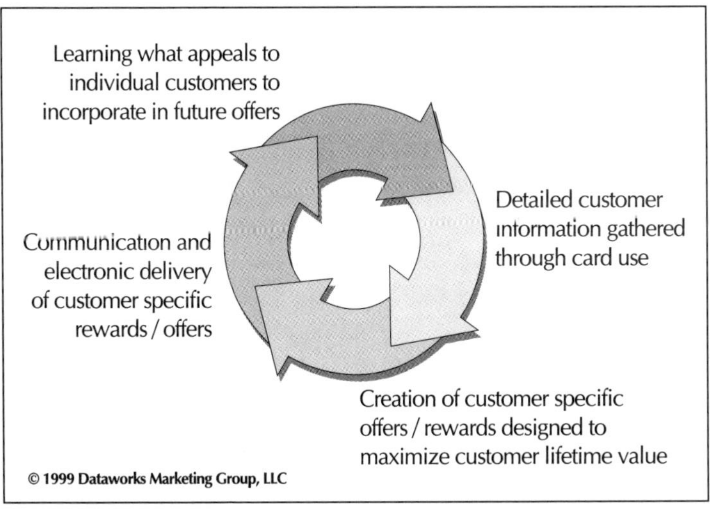

Figure 14-4

In a very real sense, the customer specific retailer is a "learning" organization.

Where to Next?

Chapter 15: Putting It All Together for Yield Management

The customer specific retail enterprise is almost complete. The technology for a retailer to operate on a customer specific level is, for the most part, here today. Thousands of retailers around the world have in place some type of database or data warehouse and are filling it with transaction level data. Some of the more advanced retailers are implementing customer specific communication vehicles, such as kiosks, web sites, etc., to communicate customer specific offers. They are then able to deliver these differentiated offers electronically at the front end.

We are almost there, but there are a few pieces that still need to be put in place for a retailer to practice true yield management. Yield management is defined here as offering different prices to different customers at different times — all designed to maximize the lifetime value and profitability of a retailer's customer base.

This is very similar to what the airlines have done. Airlines sell seats on their planes at different prices to different customers at different times; this is designed to maximize the revenue on any particular flight. It has been reported that both American and United claim annual increases in profitability of more than $100 million due to their revenue management efforts.

What is necessary to accomplish this in a retail setting? Certainly very sophisticated back room systems; ideally, expert knowledge systems that can access the vast volumes of detailed customer information on a real time basis, to determine what prices and products should be offered to which customers. This then is communicated through the tools we have already mentioned, e.g., kiosks, IVR systems, and the Internet.

Please do not dismiss this concept out of hand. As has been discussed earlier in this book, some very large retailers now have kiosk systems on line with their marketing databases and their POS systems to effect electronically communicated and delivered, customer specific offers. Expert systems are being developed to make the process that much more efficient.

First Union Corp. Bank has developed a computer system they have named "Einstein." This system is used to support their huge customer service operation. When customers call in, their information appears on the computer screen of the customer service person taking the call. Alongside the customer's name is a tiny square — red, green, or yellow. The color indicates the profitability and value of that customer to the bank. The customer service representative is much more willing to waive fees or lower credit card interest rates for a green customer, who provides healthy profits, than for a red customer, one the bank typically loses money on.

"First Union estimates its Einstein system will add at least $100 million in annual revenue. About half of that increase is expected to come from extra fees and other revenue from unprofitable customers, and from holding on to preferred customers who might otherwise leave the bank if not for the extra pampering." (*Wall Street Journal*, January 7, 1999)

In addition to the technologies and systems already discussed, there are two more pieces of the puzzle to be plugged in for true yield management in a retail setting:

1) For food retailers who sell some product by weight, a scale system supporting true customer specific retailing;
2) For any type of mass merchandise retailer, an electronic shelf tag system to support customer specific retailing.

A scale system that will support true customer specific retailing is being developed at Green Hills Farms in conjunction with Hobart. This is the next stage of evolution, after Hobart's existing scale system, which supports frequent shopper (two-tier) pricing.

In general terms, the system would work this way. A customer would learn of specific offers via a kiosk in the store or through the retailer's web site. When shopping in the produce department, the customer would place his or her selection on the self-service scale provided and use the small scanner built into the scale to scan his or her frequent shopper card. The customer's name and his or her special price or offer would be printed on the label, to be scanned and delivered at the POS.

This label could also provide additional information to the customer, such as point balance or spending toward a certain reward. In effect, this becomes a scale "kiosk" which provides the retailer with yet an additional point of communication with the customer.

Electronic shelf tags connected back to an in-store server can, with the addition of a small scanner or receiver, support customer specific pricing. Again, after learning of his or her specific offers at a kiosk, or through some other communication avenue, the customer would scan his or her card at the shelf where his or her feature item was located. The customer's name and customer specific price would be displayed on the electronic shelf tag, and would later be delivered electronically at the POS. An alternative to scanning the card at each shelf tag would be using radio frequency technology. RF chips built into the customer's frequent shopper card, detected by small receivers located on the shelf, would trigger the display to provide customer specific information.

The technology to do this is here today. It is not necessary to put such a scanner and electronic shelf tag on each of the tens of thousands of items typically carried in the average supermarket or discount store. Customer specific retailers, having full knowledge of what is occurring in their stores, can employ such a system on the 20% or so of their total items that provide them with the majority of their sales volume.

While the practicality of such a practice can (and I am sure will be!) debated, the real question becomes one of making the technology "customer friendly," so that it can be employed without asking too much of the customer. Who would have thought 10 years ago that retailers would be able to convince their customers to carry a plastic card, which the customer would have to use every time he or she shopped in order to receive the store's discounts?

It is at this point that the retailer has total control over the pricing and profit margins within the store. The customer specific retailer can now begin assembling, communicating, and delivering differentiated offers to each individual customer to maximize the lifetime value of that customer.

Consider the power of such a system. Retailers are able to communicate and deliver deals on different products to different customers. They are able to get both the loyal Coke purchasers and the loyal Pepsi purchasers to shop in the same week because they can now give customers the offers that are meaningful to them individually.

Customer specific retailers will have also learned from their extensive databases which customers are more price sensitive than others, i.e., they will have learned the price elasticity of customers. This may also be used in maximizing the yield from the customer base.

Retailers are also beginning to take the store to the customer. Many retailers are doing some type of home delivery. Customers can sit at home or in their offices and communicate with the store, learning of their special offers and doing their shopping on-line. One leading technology company is developing kiosks that can be placed in offices, allowing customers to access retailers, learn of their customer specific offers, and place orders, which will then be delivered to the place of work. This can all be personalized to the specific customer.

The next stage will be the application of predictive modeling, expert data systems, and eventually artificial intelligence, to these huge stockpiles of detailed customer information. Both RMS and SASI are already experimenting with expert systems designed to identify those new customers who offer the most potential return on investment, and will respond to specific offers. In addition, their systems are learning to identify which customers are most likely to defect; this acts as an early warning system for retailers to focus their efforts on these people in order to retain them.

Further, expert systems are being designed to assemble the offers and communications for true customer specific retailing. In effect, computers would assemble individual ads for each individual customer each week and each month, all designed to maximize the customer's lifetime value to the retailer.

Section 6: Conclusion

It is only a matter of time until customer specific retailing expands throughout many of the retail channels around the world. It is technology that is enabling this change; retailers will either embrace it or be drawn, kicking and screaming, into the future. As leading practitioners begin to personalize the shopping experience, customers will learn to expect this type of experience — and value — from others.

The customer specific retailer knows which particular brands and products are important to each of their customers, their likes and dislikes, and what additional services and privileges are important to them. As the new enterprise begins going to market this way, how long can the more traditional retailers hold out? How long can the manufacturers and packaged goods companies ignore the changing economics of the industry?

Those established retailers who ignore the Internet, and who write off home delivery, or office delivery, of products such as groceries as being only a "small niche," are doing so at their own peril. The long-term viability of some of the experiments going on today, such as Peapod or Streamline, may still be open to question. But established retailers who ignore these new business models do so at their own risk.

Too many retailers do not offer a satisfying shopping experience. How many times has the product you were looking for been out of stock? How many times have you found a dress or a suit you liked, only to find the retailer did not have your size or color preference? People today are literally starved for time; do you think they will continue to flock to stores, only to be disappointed, if they have a viable alternative?

We need only to look at the catalog industry to see how desperate customers are for alternatives to shopping in stores. My wife used to love to shop. Now, she simply orders what she likes from catalogs, and the products are delivered within a day or two to our home. The same thing for our children's clothes. Why go through the frustrating experience of dragging children from store to store to find the right sizes and colors? Simply pick up the telephone or go on-line.

Traditional self-service, mass merchandise, product based retailing is in danger. For us as retailers to survive, let alone thrive, we must change the value equation we offer our customers. Customer specific retailing, — creating a personalized retail shopping experience for our customers — may be the answer.

It is only the timing of such change that is in question; the path is not.

Conclusion

Chapter 16: The State of the Industry

So where is the retail industry today relative to frequent shopper programs? What stage are retailers at with their efforts? When will the customer specific retail enterprise be operational?

As we view the landscape today, approximately half of United States supermarkets now operate a card program. In Europe, we see retailers who are expanding existing programs, and others who are rolling out new launches. Retail card marketing programs are exploding around the world, but are they delivering bottom line results for the retailers?

For purposes of discussion, we will segment the retail industry into four groups with regard to card programs: the doubters, the dabblers, the disciples, and the devotees.

The Doubters

A number of retailers in all channels simply do not believe in card programs. They may wish to differentiate themselves by being the only retailer in their market without a card. They may think that when everyone has such a program it creates a level playing field, so why should they bother?

Certainly a number0 of these retailers are convinced that a frequent shopper program offers them no competitive advantage. They simply do not believe in it.

Historically, Every Day Low Price (EDLP) operators were among these doubters. This is rapidly changing, however, EDLP operators, such as Food Lion, launch and operate card programs. Other notable EDLP operators are exploring the benefits that card marketing may hold for them. Even traditional EDLP operators are coming to realize that all of their customers are not equal in value to them; their customer bases are made up of low-spending to high-spending customers, all offering different levels of profitability.

The Dabblers

The dabblers constitute the largest group of retailers with card programs. These are companies who have not made their card programs central or core to their operations. Many view their cards as simply another marketing program or another promotional vehicle. We see these companies launching programs as a "me too" reaction to competitive efforts.

The dabblers are characterized by having lower identification rates (the percentage of their total sales and transactions done through the card). Dabblers are typically identifying less than 80% of their turnover through their card. They are not serious about their card programs.

One problem is that many of these retailers have simply layered their card programs on top of their existing operations. In doing so, they have increased their operating expenditures without realizing any gain in profitability.

Some of these retailers are guilty of sending split messages about their card programs to their customers. For example, one retailer's ad in the United States showed several items on sale at a reduced retail price with their card, while in the next column several items were advertised at a reduced price accompanied by the phrase "no card needed." What are customers to make of this? Should they apply for and use this retailer's card or not?

The Disciples

The disciples are a much smaller group of retailers world-wide. These are companies that are capturing more than 80% of their sales, and about 60% of their transactions, through their card. They have made their card programs central to their operations and strategy.

These retailers practice differentiation among their customers, rewarding different customers with different offers or awards, based upon the customers' value to them. These companies may differentiate through a strong points program, or on price, or via a purchases program. The bottom line is that these companies are skewing the greater values to their more valuable and profitable customers.

These companies realize that what the customer sees of their card program "above the surface" is all-important. The in-store signage supporting their card program is excellent and pervasive. All their price reductions require the use of the store's frequent shopper card. They consistently run marketing programs to reinforce customers' regular shopping and spending, by offering longer-term rewards, programs such as the free Thanksgiving turkey programs in the United States, or savings certificates earned by achieving certain spending levels in defined time periods. These retailers also typically channel their community donation programs through their cards. Their goal is simple: establish their card program in the minds of their customers as one that offers tremendous value.

These are the retailers who have increased their gross profit margins by 1-2% or more, and have seen substantial improvements to their bottom lines. The increase in gross profit is a result of their redirecting their traditional markdown expense to the higher value customers, who in turn reward the retailers with even more business — offering better margins.

While these companies are having some success with their programs, they are lacking the scorecard or measurement for viewing the changes in their customer base, and for learning where their profit increases are coming from.

The Devotees

The devotees have developed just such a scorecard, the customer category management scorecard. These are the companies — and there are only a few around the world truly at this level of understanding — who now view on a regular basis the different income streams offered by their different customer groups.

They are measuring and managing their customer bases and are aligning their marketing expenditures with the different income streams to maximize their marketing investment.

These retailers are also typically able to realize savings in their traditional mass media advertising and marketing budgets. They can now measure the effect of their mass marketing efforts in a much more accurate way by using their customer information.

These retailers are at the leading edge in the evolution to true customer specific marketing. These companies are evolving their business models to a new one, based on the use of the detailed customer information generated through their card programs. Now that they can measure this new world of customer behavior, they are beginning to manage it.

To enable them to move to this new way of doing business, these companies consistently capture very high rates of information through their cards. Identifying 90% or more of sales and 75% or more of transactions week-to-week through their cards is typical of this group of retailers.

These companies see this new age of information-enabled retailing as being similar to an iceberg. What the public or the competitors see above the surface is only a small portion of the whole. The real power lies below the surface. In addition to the "above the surface" communication techniques that were described in the "Disciples" section, these retailers possess a tremendous devotion to promoting the use of this information throughout their entire organizations.

They realize that it is not enough simply to gather the detailed customer information; knowledge of how to understand it and analyze it, combined with a willingness to use it in the way they go to market, is becoming the defining competency.

These companies live and die by their detailed customer information. They measure and manage what is occurring in their customer bases. Typically, these retailers are managing both their existing customers and new customer retention. They are aware that higher-spending customers provide a substantially higher gross profit margin than lower-spending customers. And accordingly, they continually measure whether their different customer categories are growing or shrinking.

The use of this detailed customer information pervades their operations. It is pulled into customer service communications; it is used in assisting with new product selections, space management, and product category management.

It is a handful of these leading edge companies that are moving to true customer specific retailing. They have built the foundation of gathering customer information, have erected the structure of their enterprises using the new metrics, such as customer category management, and are now putting in place the technology to allow them to practice one-to-one retailing.

As we continue into the future, retail companies will evolve into two primary groups: those who are customer information literate and those who are not. The process of using detailed customer information, as generated through frequent shopper cards, to evolve a more intelligent way of doing retail business, is still in its infancy. Yes, there are immediate benefits that can accrue from a properly executed program, but the real game is much longer term. The true goal is to develop an understanding of our customers' behavior, what motivates them to shop the way they do. It is at this stage that retailers can begin to truly maximize their customer and business potential.

Conclusion

Chapter 17: Closing Thoughts

> *"The next information revolution is well under way. But it is not happening where information scientists, information executives, and the information industry in general are looking for it. It is not a revolution in technology, machinery, techniques, software, or speed. It is a revolution in CONCEPTS.*
>
> *So far, for 50 years, the information revolution has centered on data — their collection, storage, transmission, analysis, and presentation. It has centered on the "T" in IT. The next information revolution asks, What is the MEANING of information, and what is its PURPOSE? And this is leading rapidly to redefining the tasks to be done with the help of information, and with it, to redefining the institutions that do these tasks."*
>
> Peter F. Drucker

I recently purchased a new personal computer for my oldest son. We went to Dell's web site where, after responding to a few questions about how the computer was to be used, we were led through the order process. We were able to choose the processor, the amount of memory, disk size, monitor, and specify what software was to be loaded. In addition, because we had earlier told Dell that the machine would be for school/home use, Dell suggested a certain printer and scanner which we subsequently added to our order.

I next was prompted to enter my credit card information for payment, and within seconds the transaction was confirmed and assigned an order number. My son was able to track the production and shipping of his computer through Dell's web site and their connection to UPS, who delivered it. The computer was delivered to our doorstep within five days of placing the order, and it was exactly what we specified; we did not have to settle for what was on the shelf at the local computer retailer.

Consumers today are learning to expect customized services. A customer shopping at a Levi's store can now have his or her personal measurements taken by computer, and a pair of jeans, customized to the customer's figure, delivered to his or her door a few days later. The attraction of frequenting a Starbucks Coffee shop is not just the product; regular customers and their preferences are remembered. When the person behind the counter asks "The regular today, Mr. Hawkins?" he is not being facetious; the staff is trained to remember their customers' favorites. Customized service.

Charles Schwab & Co. no longer concentrates on bricks and mortar offices to build their trading business. Rather, they have made the Internet their new sales channel — and to great effect. Customers can now sit in the comfort of their own homes, *at a time convenient to them,* research stocks and mutual funds of interest to them, and place their trades and investments over their computers.

As these examples illustrate, the nature of competition is changing. Technology is enabling companies to provide a customized, individualized shopping experience. No longer is leading edge competition between products — it is between business models.

Buy.com is an Internet company shaking the world of retail to its foundations (or if not, it should be!). Buy.com is projected to do more than $600 million in sales in 1999 by selling computer equipment, software, books, videos, and electronic games at or below cost. CDs and other products are coming soon. Many of these products are sold at a loss. The company's goal is to make money by advertising to the people who visit their web site. As Scott Blum, founder of Buy.com has stated; "My goal is to reach $10 billion in revenue with 1% gross margins on product sales." Blum has created a new retail business model. How can traditional retailers compete with this?

Buy.com's prospects are not necessarily overblown Internet hyperbole; the company lists among its directors some very well known CEOs of some very large and respected companies.

Likewise, we see competition between business models occurring in other industries. Microsoft® Windows® operating system versus Sun® Microsystems's Java™

system, for example. This battle is not about specific software systems, but rather a battle of different business models for computing — PC-based or network-based.

Streamline of Boston, Massachusetts is not so much about selling groceries delivered to the home as it is about developing a different business model. They are building a relationship with a niche of customers and providing them with services to replenish their household needs of food and other staples, in addition to dealing with dry cleaning and video rentals. Streamline is not in the grocery business. They are in the customer service business; groceries just happen to be the products that they supply in satisfying their customers.

Successful companies today are not simply trying to imitate their competitors, while trying to gain some small advantage. Today's success stories are asking if there is not a better way to organize, creating a different business model, and changing the playing field.

Dell Computer has revolutionized the way companies make and market personal computers. As of March 1999, Dell was doing $14 million in daily sales through its web site, selling personal computers to companies and individuals. What did they announce they were going to do next? Dell launched a second web site, Gigabuys.com, through which they sell more than 30,000 other computer-related products. Dell already had a great following of loyal customers; with the new web site, they are now *expanding their share of customer.*

One must wonder, given the consolidation occurring in the retail industry today, with the large companies becoming even larger, if this is not the end stage in the traditional retail business model. We see the largest supermarket companies growing larger through acquisitions and mergers, all with the goal of developing similar economies of scale and logistical prowess to compete with Wal-Mart or similar competitors.

These companies run the very real risk that the world they envision will no longer be there when they finally consolidate all their acquisitions.

In a sense, there is a polarization beginning to occur in the retail industry. At one end are the product-based retailers, those who have built their entire organizations around product measurements and logistics, enabling them to go to market as "every day low price leaders". At the other end of the spectrum are those retailers who are building their organizations' core competencies on

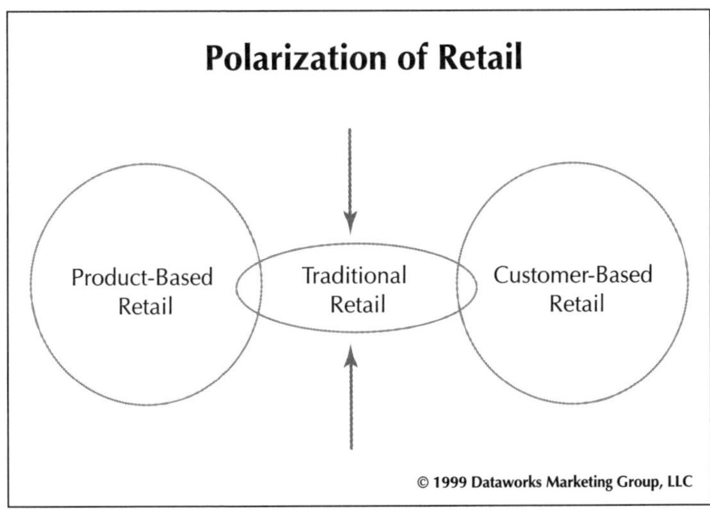

the gathering, understanding, and use of customer information, providing individualized shopping experiences to their customers. Each offers a different value equation to the customer.

Those retailers caught in the middle, undecided which way to move, will be squeezed, caught between the behemoths on one side and the customer specific retailers on the other side. This will be a battle of business models, not of products.

Recently I spent part of a day advising a start-up company attempting to develop a grocery delivery business. Their plan is to develop a relationship with a local supermarket chain, who would act as a source of supply. The delivery company believes they can bring incremental sales to the supermarket chain by delivering groceries to customers' places of work, receiving a fee from the supermarket tied to the orders' value.

This company had been working for months developing their presentation and making sales calls to different supermarket chains to get them to sign on. They had been frustrated because the supermarkets were not overly interested, most likely because of the fee structure. In a sense, the supermarket companies probably believe that they have these customers in their stores already, so why transfer their business to another channel at a lesser profit?

I suggested that this start-up company approach their business plan from a different direction. Rather than focusing on the supply side, focus on the customer side.

If they were able to approach a number of large companies in an area and sign their employees up as customers of this service, they would be in a much stronger position. Now, rather than being yet another channel for grocery distribution, they are positioning themselves as a customer service (who just happens to supply groceries).

This subtle difference in how the overall process is viewed makes a very fundamental difference in where the value lies. Before, the company would approach the supermarket saying, "We'll help you sell more of your products through our work-based delivery, and here's what it will cost you," allowing the supermarket to make only a small amount of incremental profit. Now, the company will be able to approach a supermarket and say, "We have 1,000 customers, each of whom will spend an average of $75 a week on groceries. What is this worth to you?"

The value lies in the customer portfolio, not in the products. Customer focused rather than product driven. How many retailers today, when thinking of their financial assets, would name their customers as a larger asset than their physical product inventory? Most would not even consider their customer base a financial asset — because they have not been able to measure it.

It is this fundamental concept that lies at the heart of this transition to a new way of doing retail. A retailer can now measure the value of their customer base. As they measure it, they can manage their business to it, creating new value — for themselves and for their customers.

The next few years will be a fascinating time in the retail industry around the world. Today's largest retailers are growing ever larger and more predominant, taking their product based business model global. But is this really what customers are looking for, a world full of the same stores, offering the same products, with impersonal service, in every market?

Today's technologies allow us to once again focus on our customers, to provide a personalized shopping experience for them. No longer do we have to expend our effort on the mass marketing of products to nameless customers. Now, using the data gathered through retail frequent shopper programs, we can focus on each of our customers and market to them individually. And while the information and numbers we have available are vitally important, we must remember to look beyond the facts and figures to what they are telling us about our customers. Retailers today have the opportunity to know their customers, to begin developing relationships with them, and in doing so, succeed in today's competitive marketplace. This is the goal of the customer specific retail enterprise.

Recommended Reading

I have found the following books to be particularly helpful in the development of my thinking regarding customer specific retailing.

All Consumers Are Not Created Equal
By Garth Hallberg
ISBN 0-471-12004-9/John Wiley & Sons, Inc.

Customer Specific Marketing
By Brian P. Woolf
ISBN 1-888-051-02-7/Teal Books

Managing In A Time Of Great Change
By Peter F. Drucker
ISBN 0-525-94053-7/Penguin Books USA

Mass Customization
By B. Joseph Pine II
ISBN 0-87584-372-7/Harvard Business School Press

The One To One Enterprise
By Martha Rodgers and Don Peppers
ISBN 0-385-48205-1/Doubleday

Sun Tzu and the Art of Business
By Mark McNeilly
ISBN 0-19-509996-6/Oxford University Press

The Loyalty Effect
By Frederick F. Reichheld
ISBN 0-87584-448-0/Harvard Business School Press

The Quest For Loyalty
By Frederick F. Reichheld and Scott D. Cook
ISBN 0-87584-745-5/Harvard Business Review Books

DataWorks Marketing Group, LLC

DataWorks Marketing Group works exclusively with clients who are committed to developing world-class capabilities in their understanding and use of customer data gathered through retail frequent shopper programs. The team's expertise lies in working with select retailers, wholesalers, and manufacturers throughout the world to create value and bottom line results through the utilization of detailed customer information and advanced information technology systems.

DataWorks is dedicated to operating at the leading edge in the evolution to true customer specific marketing.

DataWorks Marketing Group, LLC
P.O. Box 145 / Skaneateles, NY / 13152-0145
United States
U.S. 315.685.5282 office / U.S. 315.685.5283 fax

Visit our web site at: www.dataworksmktg.com
and contact the author at ghawkins@dataworksmktg.com

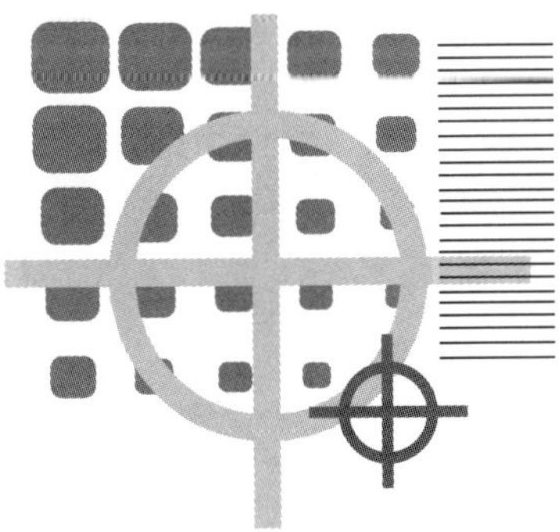

Bibliography

Peter F. Drucker, *Managing in a Time of Great Change* (New York: Penguin Books USA, Inc., 1995), p.108.

Peter F. Drucker, *Managing in a Time of Great Change* (New York: Penguin Books USA, Inc., 1995), p.109-110

Frederick F. Reichheld and Scott D. Cook, *The Quest For Loyalty* (Boston: Harvard Business Review Books, 1996), p. 16

Frederick F. Reichheld and Scott D. Cook, *The Quest For Loyalty* (Boston: Harvard Business Review Books, 1996), p. 129.

Mark McNeilly, *Sun Tzu and the Art of Business* (New York: Oxford University Press, 1996), p.19 and 21.

Rick Brooks, the *Wall Street Journal*, January 7, 1999 p.1.

Eric Nee, *Fortune* magazine, March 29, 1999, p. 120.

Brian P. Woolf, *Measured Marketing, A Tool to Shape Food Store Strategy*, The Coca-Cola Retailing Research Council, 1994.

Index

Introductory Note: Page numbers including a "t" refer to a table.